LEAP OF FAITH

FREE TRADE AND THE FUTURE OF CANADA

Hurtig Publishers
Edmonton

Hurtig Publishers Ltd.
10560 – 105 Street
Edmonton, Alberta
Canada T5H 2W7

Canadian Cataloguing in Publication Data
Laxer, James, 1941-
  Leap of Faith

  ISBN 0-88830-298-3 (bound). — ISBN
0-88830-297-5 (pbk)

  1. Tariff — Canada.   2. Canada — Economic
policy — 1971-*   3. Canada — Foreign economic
relations — United States.   I. Title.
HF1766.L39 1986   382.7'1'0971   C86-091294-9

Printed and bound in Canada
by Friesen Printers

Contents

To Jonathan

Chapter One

The Free Trade Debate
Is About Sovereignty

In late September 1985, Prime Minister Brian Mulroney telephoned U.S. President Ronald Reagan to request the opening of formal trade talks between Canada and the United States. The initiative was historic. The Progressive Conservative government had turned its back on a century of Conservative tradition to seek a deal with Washington for the purpose of removing virtually all trade barriers between the two countries.

Much more was at stake than in any normal commercial deal. Proponents and opponents alike recognized that the project had immense implications for the future of Canada.

This book examines the wisdom of the government's economic strategy. The federal government has two basic economic policies, free trade with the United States and, related to that, the encouragement of further foreign investment in Canada. They are based on a single underlying assumption, that Canada needs to move away from its mixed economy toward a more "market-driven" economy, to use the phrase employed by the Macdonald Commission.

The thesis of this book is that the basic economic policies of the Mulroney government will do Canada more harm than good, and that the underlying assumption is an anachronism that involves a misreading of how successful economies work in the late twentieth century.

Despite its importance to all Canadians, the debate about free trade in Canada is being conducted as though it is a matter

1

for the experts alone. Long, dry dissertations peppered with professional jargon on seemingly arcane matters can convince most people that the debate is either beyond them or that it is safely being conducted by those who understand it. This is a very dangerous position for Canadians to adopt. The free trade debate will have a marked impact on the careers, communities, and life-style of all Canadians. It may even determine, as Quebec Premier Robert Bourassa has suggested, whether Canada will continue to exist as a sovereign nation.

It is especially dangerous to leave the free trade debate to economists, allowing them to make what amount to political and ethical choices, wrapped up in the theorems of neo-classical economics. The Canadian debate about free trade is not primarily a debate about economics. Economists should not be allowed to dominate the discussion and to pretend that only they have the expertise to understand the complex issues that are at stake.

There is a dirty little secret that everyone should know about most economists in Canada. For a large number of economists, who accept the neo-classical faith (about which more later), Canada has always been a blot on the economic landscape, a monstrosity that should be put out of its misery as soon as possible.

Having accused economists of harbouring dark feelings about Canada, one must add at once that, from their point of view, these feelings make perfect sense. Canada's economic history over the past two centuries amounts to a protracted defiance of accepted economic theory. Instead of letting the free play of the market determine everything, a policy which would have drawn us into economic union with the United States long ago, Canadians have opted for the alternative course of tying a nation together on the northern half of North America. For decades, Canadian economic literature has been peppered with denunciations of this choice.

The dominant strain of economic thought in Canada is called neo-classical economics. It is an economic school which operates on a number of key premises. Only by understanding the premises can we understand the conclusions reached by its practitioners. Neo-classical economics is based, in the end, on the theory that human beings are "marginal utility maximiz-ers"—that they make rational economic choices, based on a c. understanding of their best interests. The "economic man offers what he, or she, has in the market-place. Offerings may ke the form of labour, professional knowledge, capital, land rent, etc. The market will put a price on the offerings. In the e and competitive market-place, each individual will compete ith every other. The result will be the fastest possible growth c a productive and economically efficient society.

From this model, the impl tions of the benefits of the market system naturally flow. In society, populated by economic individuals, the market respo to their wishes with a subtlety that is far superior to what can chieved by any planning mechanism. In the end, the market sys n guarantees freedom for all, because through it people can bu and sell, offering their skills and assets, and reaping rewards.

The untrammelled market system is the highest ideal as far as neo-classical economics is concerned. Anything that stands in the way of competition is a market imperfection that should, if possible, be eliminated. Monopolies and undue power for trade unions are two examples of market imperfections. There is another one, which is crucial to this discussion: the nation state. Naturally, in a world of self-determining utility maximizers, there is little logic in allowing the market system to be blocked by the existence of national frontiers. For this reason, neo-classical economists oppose trade barriers between nations and have always favoured free trade. Free trade would allow each country to do the things it does best. According to this notion of "comparative advantage," the market system operating across international frontiers will automatically allocate tasks to different peoples according to their aptitudes. Some nations will manufacture, others will grow food, and others will sell services and train neo-classical economists.

Canada stands convicted before the court of neo-classical economic thought for two repeated and basic crimes: the use of the state to achieve economic development on a significant scale; and the attempt to do certain things in Canada as part of a strategy of nation-building, quite apart from the dictates of the market system. Most Canadians have gone quietly about their lives unaware that their country has been the site of such crimes against economics.

Having understood that Canada is the scene of heinous outrages against economic theory, Canadians may be considerably relieved to learn that neo-classical theory is itself a dubious proposition, whose central tenets are now under attack by some of the world's most brilliant economists. In a luminous book, MIT economist Lester Thurow critiques the prevailing mode in economics, what he calls "equilibrium price-auction" analysis. He states:

> ...the discipline of economics is on its way to becoming a guild. Members of a guild, as we know, tend to preserve and advance traditional theories rather than try to develop new ways of thinking and doing things to solve new problems. The equilibrium price-auction view of the world is a traditional view with a history as old as that of economics itself: the individual is asserted to be a maximizing consumer or producer within free supply-demand markets that establish an equilibrium price for any kind of goods or service. This is an economics blessed with an intellectual consistency, and one having implications that extend far beyond the realm of conventional economic theory. It is, in short, also a political philosophy, often becoming something approaching a religion.[1]

The reason we must understand the limitations of neo-classical theory is that the case for free trade in Canada is based on it. The studies done for the Economic Council of Canada, the Macdonald Commission, the Ontario Economic Council, and the C. D. Howe Institute that favour free trade reach their conclusions, not through broad consideration of the national interest, but through the application of neo-classical assumptions to models of the Canadian economy which, naturally enough, lead to results based on those assumptions. If the assumptions are wrong, so too are the conclusions.

The federal government has told Canadians that it has a long list of studies that prove the value of free trade, that its case is based on hard evidence. It is important to examine this claim, since its message to Canadians is that they should sit back and let the econometricians with their mathematical models and their computer programs decide the future for us.

The federal government speaks of these studies as though they have been carried out by a priesthood that is beyond challenge. What it is telling us is that today's economics is a science, whose theorems and conclusions are a reliable guide to the future. In reality, all over the world, societies are learning just how fallible the so-called "science" of economics is.

If we look at their track-record at predicting how their medicine will affect society, we can see that economists have no more ability to assess the future than have medicine men the ability to cure disease. Today's economics is flawed; its predictions are increasingly meaningless; its depictions of the world are ever more distant from reality. Over the past two decades, mainstream economists have made important predictions that have been wrong—not wrong in degree, but massively wrong. For example, many economists in the 1960s believed that they had found the key to evening out the economic cycle so that acceptable trade-offs could be made between unemployment and inflation. Then came the 1970s, with its combination of simultaneous high unemployment and high inflation—stagflation—and economic orthodoxy was in trouble.

In its ninth annual review in 1972, the Economic Council of Canada made an extensive series of forecasts about the country's economy to the beginning of the 1980s, making use of a highly sophisticated econometric model. It predicted that unemployment would be easing as Canada entered the 1980s and would likely be less than 4 per cent. Just to cover all possibilities, the Economic Council gave a less optimistic prediction, based on the assumption of lower economic growth abroad, in which case Canadian unemployment would range between 4 and 5 per cent in 1980.[2] Actually, unemployment in 1980 turned out to be 7.5 per cent—much more serious than the Economic Council predicted.[3]

Again in Canada, a federal government report in 1973, reflecting the orthodoxy of the day, forecast a huge increase in the country's ability to produce oil and natural gas, at very low prices.[4] The prediction was made meaningless within a few months by the world oil price revolution at the end of 1973. And, the same orthodoxy could not foresee the risk of falling international oil prices in September 1981 when experts for both the federal and Alberta governments signed an agreement on petroleum revenues that did not even mention the possibility of a price drop.

In listing these important failures, the point is not that orthodox economists are alone in being unable to forecast the future. Economic developments are affected by a baffling array of factors: demographic changes, altered work habits, movements for political reform, and political and technological revolutions. One cannot expect economists to predict women's liberation, the pill, the microchip, or Islamic fundamentalism, but all of these will have an impact on the world they are attempting to reduce to a series of mathematical models.

Economic models are important. The more limited the nature of the forecasts in both time and scale, the more accurate the results can be. However, economic models have turned out to be woefully inadequate when it comes to making broad predictions about the fate of a whole society over a long period of time. The fact is that debates about the future must involve the insights of many disciplines. When choices about the whole future direction of a society are being made, as is the case with free trade, we should recognize, at the outset, that the exercise is not one in which econometric models can produce "scientific forecasts."

Many of the best economists are now recognizing that economics needs inputs from other disciplines and that it must alter its perception of humanity to fit reality, even if that plays havoc with aesthetically pleasing models. Economics now is nearing what can be called a paradigm shift. A paradigm shift occurs when the theorems of a science are unable to order reality acceptably. At such a time in the history of the science, the true believers defend the old paradigm with greater and greater fanaticism, explaining away anomolies that threaten to expose the old way of doing things.

Paradigm shifts occur in every science. They have about them the horror and fascination of revolutions. An old theory of the world becomes ever less able to explain reality. A period of chaos ensues, and finally a new paradigm emerges. Today's economics is entering an age of chaos. Its high priests are speaking a language, ever more intricate, that only they can understand.

Behind the façade of technical expertise, economics suffers from very real problems in terms of its central assumptions. Those assumptions concern the nature of the individual and society. The "human being" at the centre of economic theory is "economic man," a creature who inhabits an atomistic world of solitary people who come together to form groupings for various purposes to pursue their self-interest.

"Economic man" is descended from what we might call "Lockean man," the mythical creature upon whom the great documents of the American Revolution, the Declaration of Independence, and the U.S. Constitution are based. No other social science would pay serious attention to this hypothetical creature in the late twentieth century. And yet, "economic man" is still at the centre of economics.

The result is that economics is unable to come to grips with key developments in today's global political economy. It is especially weak when it comes to dealing with the modern state, multinational corporations, and power relationships within and between societies. To put it simply, an economics that does not understand politics has little ability to make judgements about the real world.

Just what conclusions have been reached by the most extensive, and presumably most persuasive, of the free trade studies, the Macdonald Commission report?[5] The Macdonald Commission concluded that with a comprehensive free trade deal with the United States, Canada's gross national product (GNP) would increase eventually by between 3 and 8 per cent—not each year, of course, but once only by an overall amount of between 3 and 8 per cent. Drawing conclusions about the economic growth that would be generated by a free trade deal with the United States, the commissioners stated "...on the basis of analyses made for this Commission by competent professionals, we are prepared to say it would be in the order of a 3 to 8 per cent increase of our national income."[6]

The "leap of faith" supported by Donald Macdonald amounts to an invitation to Canadians to reach out for what we might call that 8 per cent bonus. Based on the track-record of Canada's neo-classical economics practitioners, however, we are as likely to end up with a 3 to 8 per cent decrease of our GNP as an increase.

The 8 per cent carrot that is being held in front of us is really only part of the question. There are fundamental issues at stake in the free trade debate that take us far beyond the models that have been worked up to show us the advantages of a free trade arrangement with Washington.

The free trade debate is about whether Canadians really want their country to continue in more than a symbolic way. We have been building up to this decision for a very long time. In the next five years, we will make a choice that will matter for generations to come. All Canadians, not just the experts, had better get involved in choosing.

The report of the Macdonald Commission on the Canadian economy has come down strongly on behalf of a comprehensive free trade deal with the United States. Hard on the heels of the report, the Mulroney government has undertaken an initiative to achieve such a deal. It is no exaggeration to say that the fate of this undertaking will have more to do with determining the shape of Canada for decades to come than any other decision we have made as a nation in the twentieth century.

The Macdonald Commission and the Mulroney government have been seized of a single and simple "truth": that Canada's economy needs the discipline of a much larger secured market if it is to become internationally competitive and if it is to shed public-sector interference and approach the ideal of an unfettered free enterprise system. The means of achieving this change is to negotiate a comprehensive free trade deal with the United States for the removal of all significant barriers to trade—of both the tariff and non-tariff varieties.

While the details of Canada's free trade initiative will only become fully known as formal negotiations with the United States proceed, the broad outline of the project is already clear. There are three models for possible bilateral trade agreements between Canada and the United States: sectoral trade deals; the establishment of a Canadian-American free trade area; and the creation of a common market involving the two countries. It is apparent that the large majority of advocates of free trade in Canada favour the second model, a free trade area. They reject the first option, sectoral trade deals, both because they prefer a broader arrangement and because they believe that the United States has little interest in further agreements along the lines of the Canada-U.S. Auto Pact. They also reject the notion of a common market, in which Canada and the United States would have a single and integrated trading relationship with the rest of the world. Instead, they opt for a free trade area, which would allow both the United States and Canada to continue to have separate trading arrangements with other countries.

Just how would the free trade area work? The free trade area would involve the comprehensive abolition of trade barriers between Canada and the United States, both of the tariff and non-tariff variety. It would result in a harmonized and integrated continental economy in which Canadian-American trade would be overseen by a joint non-political trade commission, which would arbitrate disagreements about the trading relationship. Canadian free traders hope that Canada can negotiate an agreement that would allow for a long transitional period during which the smaller Canadian economy would be able to adjust to complete free trade. (It should be pointed out that the hope of Canadian free traders for a long transitional period to phase in the agreement is not shared by American officials. William Merkin, the number two American official in the bilateral talks with Canada, commented in February 1986 that as a general rule the U.S. Congress will refuse to give firms in Canada "a head start" by allowing them more time than firms in the United States to adjust to the agreement.[7])

This book looks at the wisdom of the proposed free trade project. It is about the radical conclusions that the Macdonald Commission and the Mulroney government have reached. For, indeed, as we will see in later chapters, what is proposed would radically alter the way we live our lives in Canada, bringing us much closer in our practices and customs to those in the United States.

The Canadian government has chosen an odd moment to act on the free trade issue. It has sought negotiations at a time when Canada has been enjoying record high trade surpluses with the United States. In 1984 that surplus totalled $20 billion, in 1985 $20.4 billion, higher on a per capita basis than Japan's trade surplus with the United States. To act now is to ensure that American attention will be focussed on bringing down the Canadian surplus, at the expense of jobs in Canada. But much more is involved than these short-term considerations.

It makes sense for us to begin the discussion by looking at what the Reagan administration wants from Canada in a trade deal.

U.S. negotiators will obviously not be acting to perpetuate Canada's large trade surplus—quite the reverse. Aside from the immediate issue of the trade balance, two considerations will motivate them. One is the effect a deal with Canada could have on America's other trading partners, a demonstration that, unhappy with the trading practices of others, the United States is prepared to place greater emphasis on commerce in its own neighbourhood. The second motive is to get rid of Canadian public practices that restrain the full operation of the market north of the border.

This second motive gets at the crux of the matter. The debate has very little to do with tariffs. When most people think about barriers to trade, they think about tariffs, the traditional form of barrier. Tariffs, as everyone knows, have long been collected on imported goods as a way of raising the price of imports to give domestic production an edge in the home market. But tariffs have been coming down. As a member of the General Agreement on Tariffs and Trade (GATT), Canada has participated in all of the general rounds of tariff reduction since the late 1940s. The most recent GATT round, the so-called Tokyo Round, was completed in 1979. Under the schedule agreed to, tariffs were to be sharply reduced in eight equal steps from January 1, 1980, to January 1, 1987. By the end of the process, Canada's tariff on dutiable industrial goods was to drop from just over 14 per cent to just over 9 per cent. Of greatest importance to the present discussion, by 1987 80 per cent of Canadian exports to the United States will enter duty-free.

Tariffs are now vestigial. They remain important only in marginal industries. The real issue is non-tariff barriers, such as regional tax incentives, government procurement policies, the treatment of foreign-owned firms, and the setting of currency exchange rates. These are the tools used in advanced industrial countries to pursue industrial strategies. The problem is that they are also the key measures employed by nations to maintain favourable trade balances with competitors. Dividing the domestic impact of such measures from their support for exports is very difficult indeed. These tools are central to the economic power of the modern state, the key to sovereignty in the late twentieth century, just as tariffs were in the nineteenth.

Although the United States has used plenty of non-tariff measures over the years, such as the Buy America Act and the Domestic International Sales Corporations (DISC), it has relied less on the notion of public-private partnership to achieve an industrial strategy than have other developed countries. Most Americans have believed in the market system to divide economic winners from losers and to assure growth. They favour what has been called the "level playing field" when it comes to trade, a fair and equal chance in the market-place for all competitors. This attitude has been quite natural for a country like the United States, both because of its non-interventionist economic philosophy and because its vast population makes this stance inherently advantageous for itself.

People with interventionist philosophies in other countries do not see things the same way. Canada, in particular, has developed through a mix of private and public-sector partnership different from the United States. In part, this has been a response to the challenge of developing a country larger in area than the United States, with one-tenth its population. The result has been an economy where government-owned airlines, railways, oil companies, and broadcasting and telephone companies operate alongside the private sector. The idea of public-sector involvement in economic development is not anathema in Canada, and has deep roots in the Canadian tradition.

It makes sense to underline the seemingly innocuous phrase "level playing field." It is a code phrase that reveals much about the American agenda for free trade talks that will attempt to reorder the Canadian economy to operate along American lines, to the benefit of U.S.-based corporations. The phrase "level playing field" is often linked to the other key American phrase "everything on the table." U.S. negotiators have insisted that the talks not be limited in any way at the outset. Peter Murphy, when he was about to be appointed chief U.S. negotiator for the talks with Canada, reiterated the American insistence that everything be on the table, including cultural policies. Murphy commented on the Canadian desire that certain issues be set aside, particularly in the cultural area: "The more talk of that, the less incentive there is for us."[8]

The American demand that "everything be on the table" is ominous for Canada precisely because it points up the enormous asymmetry between the two countries. Since the United States is a global superpower in which many of the world's leading multinational corporations are based, the sinews of its nationhood are not even touched in a set of negotiations with Canada. For Canada, a much smaller country with a uniquely large proportion of its economy owned by those American multinationals, the reverse is true. When we put the two American code phrases together, while keeping in mind the essential difference between the United States and Canada, it is evident that what is being negotiated is precisely the limits that will be placed on Canadian sovereignty in exchange for access to the U.S. market.

The proposed free trade agreement can best be understood as a formalized bargain between Canada and the United States. As everyone knows, there are two sides to every bargain. What the Canadian free traders want is complete and assured access to the American market for Canadian producers. In return for that access they will limit Canadian economic sovereignty, to lock Canada into the larger pattern of the American economy, to discard Canadian ways of doing things in favour of American ways of doing things. Limiting sovereignty, whether advertently or inadvertently, means, quite simply, limiting future choices; that is why it is so important to take such steps only with very great care. Once made, the free trade bargain will not be unmade. It will be more important to Canadians than their own national constitution in determining what they can do and not do as a society. This book is about the proposed bargain, its potential impact on Canada, and the alternatives to it.

Before we can make sense of the proposed bargain, we need to look back briefly at where the free-trade debate came from. Why are Canadians going through a national debate on free trade, an issue that many people had thought was settled decades ago? It is true that there has always been a current of opinion in Canada in favour of a general free trade agreement with the United States. However, before the Mulroney government came to office in September 1984, no government, either Liberal or Conservative, was prepared to reopen the great free trade debate of 1911 in all of its dimensions.

While the coming to power of the Mulroney Conservatives put into place a government ideologically inclined to much closer relations with the United States, it was not the election of the PC government alone that has led to the current free trade debate.

In a wider sense, the free trade debate of the 1980s is the product of a decade and a half of uncertainty and frustration in Canadian economic policy-making that reflects the serious structural problems of the Canadian economy. Since 1970, the Canadian economy has exhibited chronic problems of a basic kind that have continued to be present during alternating periods of expansion and recession. In other words, the problems of the economy have been more than a simple matter of moderating the economic cycle to keep recessions from being too severe and to make sure that periods of expansion do not lead to excessive inflation and supply shortages.

Recognition that the Canadian economy faces chronic difficulties has grown since the beginning of the 1970s. Depending on their perspective, people have focussed on different aspects of the problem—high unemployment, the dislocation brought about due to technological revolution, and the consequences of increasing competition with East Asian economies.

All of these problems were felt during the 1970s. But it was the brutal consequences of the recession of 1981-82 that created general anxiety about the Canadian economy.

The recession was the worst since the Great Depression of the 1930s. From June 1981 to December 1982, Canada experienced the most severe economic contraction of any industrialized country, much more serious, for example, than that in the United States. Real gross national product declined by 7 per cent in Canada compared with 3 per cent in the United States. Industrial production dropped by a shocking 18 per cent in Canada, compared with 12 per cent in the United States.

The recession took a heavy toll throughout Canadian society. Young people coming into the job market found themselves facing the stone wall of unemployment. Between January 1981 and December 1982, the number of jobs held by young men (aged fifteen to twenty-four) fell by 272,000. The unemployment rate for young men soared from 13.5 per cent to 24.0 per cent. Between the peak of employment in 1981 and the trough in 1982, 321,000 jobs were lost in the nation's goods-producing industries, 194,000 of these in the manufacturing sector. Business bankruptcies reached record-breaking levels. Every part of the country was affected, from Newfoundland, where real levels of unemployment (including discouraged workers) climbed far past 20 per cent, to Alberta where the petroleum boom ended and unemployment jumped past 10 per cent.

While recovery began in 1983, and has continued since, the numbing truth has come home to Canadians that the country will not return to anything like full employment for the foreseeable future. The severe recession of 1981-82 magnified the sense of growing problems in the Canadian economy and helped to generate the great national debate about economic strategy, a debate in which free trade is so central.

Whether Canada should pursue free trade with the United States or not turns on the underlying strategic question which has emerged about the Canadian economy: how can Canada achieve international competitiveness in the late twentieth century? All concerned with the national debate that is now underway agree that this is the essential question. Where they differ concerns the answers to this question.

Free traders want Canadians to emulate the American economic model. Their conclusion that free trade with the United States is the best option for the country rests on the assumption that the American market system is the highest expression of what is possible in an economy. They hope that by linking Canada with the vibrant U.S. economy, fresh air will course through the musty corridors of Canadian enterprise, calling people in this country to meet the challenge of competition by rising to new heights of entrepreneurial energy.

It is not unfair to the free traders to say that in things economic they prefer the American way of doing things to the Canadian. They hope that free trade will help move Canadians away from their mixed economy to one in which the market system will be stronger.

Since for the free traders the assumption that the American economic model is an ideal toward which Canadians should move is key to their position on trade, we will examine the American economic model in the next two chapters.

Chapter Two

America's Industrial Economy: In Decline

For me, the story of what has been happening to America's industrial economy is most graphically felt in South Chicago, where I met Frank Lumpkin.[9]

Frank Lumpkin has his office in the small second-floor quarters of the Save Our Jobs Committee. He has been fighting on behalf of thirty-five hundred workers in South Chicago who lost their jobs in 1980 when Wisconsin Steel shut down.

With him in the office are other men in their late sixties, thirty-year men, who spent their working lives in the now silent steel mill. Lumpkin, a black born in Georgia, has lived in Chicago since the 1940s. Two fingers on his left hand are missing, evidence of the hard life that he has led in the mill. Lumpkin is a natural leader—eloquent, calm, and resilient. He has fought for the benefits of the workers and still hopes that someday at least part of the plant will be reopened.

Downstairs, the owner of the restaurant and bar is suffering because Lumpkin and his fellow steel-workers have lost their jobs. He figures he will soon be out of business. For an entire community in South Chicago, the clock stopped on the day when the last pay-cheques handed the workers bounced on a stop-payment order issued by the Chase Manhattan Bank.

Driving across South Chicago, I can see that the story of Frank Lumpkin and his co-workers has been repeated many times over. The heart of the American steel industry, concentrated in the south end of Chicago and extending east across the state line into Indiana, is dying. All of Chicago, while far from death, is a monument to the passing of American industrial prowess. It is the great American city of the mid-twentieth century, a city based on industries that are now on the wane.

The decline of the industrial heartland of the United States is a poignant reminder that the American economy has very deep problems in the late twentieth century. And let us not forget, it is to this declining industrial heartland that the free traders would tie Canada's industrial centre.

The fate of South Chicago, Cleveland, Buffalo, and other industrial cities in the United States is actually a symptom of the most important economic development of our epoch—the passing of the United States from the summit of global economic mastery. It is important for us to step back and contemplate its significance. Throughout our entire history, Canadians have watched the growth of the United States to ever greater power. At the end of the Second World War, we lived beside a nation that had achieved greater economic sway than any country in history. Now, for the first time, Canadians are watching the decline of the United States vis-à-vis the rest of the world economy. For us this is not so much an economic as a cultural shock of profound importance. We need to get our bearings in this changed world of the late twentieth century.

The decline of the United States can be seen in raw numbers: the rise of a trade deficit that reached $150 billion a year in 1985; the return of the United States to the status of a debtor nation in 1985 for the first time since World War I, with a net debt that will reach $1 trillion by 1990; the decline of the United States from producing 50 per cent of the world's economic output in 1945, to 25 per cent by the mid-1980s, on the way to 16 per cent by the end of the century; and the projection that Japan will pass America in per capita national income in the first decade of the next century.

The Border States of America

While the United States as a whole is declining in global

18

terms, what matters more to Canadians is what has been happening to regions of the United States closest to Canada.

The hit film *Beverly Hills Cop* gives us a glimpse of two civilizations that exist side by side in the United States. There is the clean, rich, high-tech land of Beverly Hills and there is the dirty, broken-down frightening ruin of Detroit. Eddie Murphy plays the film's hero, the street-smart cop from Detroit who has a thing or two to show the ultra-modern police in Beverly Hills. It is a perfect example of what Alvin Toffler would call the third-wave, electronic world being confronted by the second-wave smokestack, industrial past.

In its way the film suggests something important to Canadians who are now considering the proposition of free trade with the United States. In discussions of free trade, we usually think of the United States as a homogeneous entity—a country with ten times our population, and an enormous market. What we routinely fail to do is to see the United States for what it is, an immensely diverse country with some regions rising and representing the future and other regions declining and representing the past.

The problem for Canadians is a simple one: between us and the prosperous regions of the United States, lies a land of decline, and rust, and failing industries. If we define this land to include all of the states that border on Canada—let us call it the Border States of America (BSA)—we can get some idea of the human story that has been unfolding close to us in the northern tier of the neighbouring republic. The border states are more similar to Canada than any other region. Their experience may tell us what to expect if we have free trade with the United States.

Thirteen American states border on Canada. Stretching from Maine in the east to Washington in the west (and Alaska in the Northwest), the Border States of America have a combined population of just over sixty-two million people—about the size of West Germany.[10] Four of the states predominate—New York, Pennsylvania, Ohio, and Michigan.

For the past fifteen years the Border States of America have had an economic and social record of decline and blight in comparison both to the more prosperous regions to the south and to Canada to the north.

During the first half of this decade, the thirteen states in the BSA increased their population by only 1.05 per cent, a dismal showing next to the 4 per cent increase for the United States as a whole. In dramatic contrast, three states—Florida, Texas, and California—accounted for half the total increase in population in the country. The Big Three added 5.5 million people to their population, while the thirteen states in the BSA added a scant seven hundred thousand. While Ohio and Michigan were actually declining in population, Texas was adding 2.2 million to its population, with a 15.2 per cent rate of increase during the half decade. (Because of declining world oil prices after 1982 and the very sharp plunge in prices in the winter of 1986, the Texas economy is now facing its own severe problems.)

What accounted for the sharply different growth rates in the BSA and in the Big Three was the huge migration of Americans from the border states to the sun belt. The migration led not only to a shift in population but to a new alignment in wealth, industrial location, and political power as well. The numbers for total income tell the story. Between 1970 and 1983, total real income (adjusted for inflation) of the United States increased by just over 47 per cent. In the border states, however, total income increased by only 28 per cent—compared to 95 per cent in Florida. By comparison, Canada's aggregate real income grew by just over 48 per cent during the same period, a fraction more than the United States, but sharply more than the border states. In addition, Canada's population grew at over four times the rate of the border states during the first half of the 1980s, increasing by about 1 per cent a year, for an addition of over 1 million people.[11]

These population and income figures point to significant underlying changes. South of the BSA, a new America has been emerging—one in which the traditional smokestack industries like auto and steel play a much less important role, in which unions are much less powerful, in which the service industries predominate. Increasingly, this new America is buying its industrial products from Japan, West Germany, and the newly industrializing countries (and Canada), while allowing the industries of the border states to lapse into decline.

In recent years, the economic policies of the U.S. government have been particularly unfavourable to the border states. Reaganomics has involved a hybrid of runaway government spending with tight money and high interest rates. This combination of policies has attracted a record inflow of foreign investment to the United States, an inflow which has driven up the value of the American dollar. The overvalued U.S. dollar has contributed mightily to the growth of a $150 billion annual trade deficit for the country. Americans have been able to buy imports dirt-cheap, while they have had enormous difficulty selling their own products abroad. While these U.S. policies have helped promote industrial expansion abroad (including Canada), they have priced American industrial products not only out of international markets, but out of the U.S. market as well.

Over the past fifteen years a vast American region, which was once the industrial centre of the global economy, has experienced sharp decline. Today Japanese and Korean steel can be sold profitably at the gates of the U.S. Steel Company in Pittsburgh.

Canadians need to understand what has happened to the Border States. We live north of them and the contrast between their experience and ours could not be clearer. Canada's population has continued to grow, and despite the sharpness of the 1981-82 recession here, our economic growth has compared well to that of other economies. (In 1985, the Canadian economy grew faster than the U.S. economy as a whole.)

The quite different long-term economic performance of Canada and the border states is a complex phenomenon. The decline of the Canadian dollar against its American counterpart since the mid-1970s has helped make our exports to the United States more competitive. Beyond that, what stands out is the contrast between Canadian and American social and economic policies. While the United States has always valued mobility and migration as the appropriate responses to changing economic times, Canadians have emphasized the preservation of existing communities through a whole host of government programs, including equalization payments. Now that fate has passed the border states by, millions of Americans have simply moved south to the more prosperous regions of their country.

But where does that leave Canadians? It leaves us on the wrong side of a southward shifting centre of economic power on the continent.

Full free trade with the United States would involve the harmonization of our economic policies with those of the United States. Canadian economic sovereignty, in the sense of the pursuit of a separate economic strategy, would be a thing of the past. Why, we must ask, would Canada do better than have the Border States of America? Is not their fate a warning to us? If the BSA had had its own national government, separate from the rest of the United States, would it have fared so badly, or would it have designed policies that made sense for its survival? In the end, is the difference between the performance of the border states and that of Canada not, in part, the measure of the worth of economic sovereignty?

The decline of the Border States of America is a traumatic contemporary event. To put its fate into perspective, it helps to stand back and take a longer look at the process of industrial decline. One of the best places in the world to do that is in the valleys around Manchester, England, where the first industrial revolution began two centuries ago. Here the early inventions that allowed for mechanized production in the textile industry were made. By the early nineteenth century, fabrics produced in the factories near Manchester were exported to markets around the world. A new industrial civilization had been born. The city of Manchester became the proud symbol of industrial Britain and was second only to London in importance. A new school of economics, the Manchester school, that preached laissez-faire and free trade, came into being.

But the advantages Britain had in being first in the industrial revolution brought in their train disadvantages for the future. British industrialists learned lessons from their early success that made things harder for them later on. British industry tended to be undercapitalized and its system of work haphazard and disorganized by the standards of countries such as the United States and Germany that industrialized after Britain. Having been first, and having enjoyed the fruits of worldwide markets at the beginning of the industrial age, British industry has suffered ever since.

Today, the United States is beginning to suffer from similar problems, as its industry ceases to be the most productive in the world.

The quarter century following the Second World War was an extraordinary period in global economic history. For the first time since the days of British supremacy in the mid-Victorian era, one country, the United States, dominated the world economy. The industrial economies of Western Europe and Japan were in ruins as a result of the war.

The great underlying fact of the post-war economy was that huge markets existed for the re-building of western Europe and Japan, as well as for the satisfaction of consumer demand in North America, which had been held down by depression in the 1930s and war in the 1940s.

Buttressed by international economic institutions such as the World Bank, the International Monetary Fund (IMF), and the General Agreement on Tariffs and Trade (GATT), all established during the war and in its immediate aftermath, the industrial world underwent the longest and deepest economic expansion ever. With only mild dips along the way, expansion continued until the end of the 1960s. This was the great age of what we can now call the "old tech," the smokestack industries—auto, steel, electrical products—that made the U.S. Northeast and Midwest the industrial powerhouse of the world. U.S. productivity increases and reinvestment in manufacturing capability were high—a stark contrast to the dismal performance that was to come later.

The foundations of the American economic system were these: huge markets for the standardized products of the "old tech"; the expansion of American multinationals abroad in pursuit of resources and markets; the use of the U.S. dollar as the reserve currency of the non-Communist world; and, under the auspices of GATT, the rolling back of trade barriers and the steady achievement of freer trade.

America's productive superiority guaranteed the United States a regular surplus in merchandise trade, both for agricultural and industrial commodities; flowing out were U.S. dollars to pay for the extension of American direct investment abroad and to fund America's world-wide military establishment.

The key thing to grasp is that it was the exceptional nature of the post-war period that led to the immense success of the system. Regrettably, this meant that the lessons learned during these years would become more the basis for myths in the future than for useful guidance for economic policy.

The job that was being done during these years, as has been mentioned, was the satisfaction of consumer demand that had been held down during the Depression and the war, and the rebuilding of the industrial plant of Western Europe and Japan. To do this job, the American economic plant had only to gear up and run. The huge increases in productive capability achieved during the war were in place to provide the engine for the post-war economic miracle.

For American enterprises, the lesson seemed to be that their supremacy was natural and came easily. Their production methods and system of product development were mythologized to the point of being virtually beyond criticism.

Both at the level of the individual firm and at the level of government macroeconomic policy, the lessons of the post-war age were misleading. At the level of the firm, the lesson was that production would take care of itself—therefore, the place to concentrate managerial effort was on the financial side of the corporation. At the level of the economy as a whole, the lesson was much the same. The prodigious productive machine would deliver the goods. Therefore, the job of government was to fine-tune aggregate demand to keep the economy running at full throttle. Years later, business managers, politicians, and trade union leaders would learn the wrong lessons from this. "It worked then, why not now?," they would lament in the tough years after 1970.

Then two things happened simultaneously. The pent-up demand for consumer durables (cars, television sets, and household appliances) was being met, and productive capacity to meet it was increasing prodigiously. As the Western European and Japanese industrial systems were rebuilt, a greatly enlarged capacity to meet consumer demand became available. It was inevitable under these circumstances that the American firms that had enjoyed huge markets and little effective competition at the beginning of the era would be facing shrinking markets and rising competition at its end.

In the long term, in industrial economies achievement of a given set of economic tasks, by definition, results in reduced demand for these same tasks. Such reduced demand must eventually result in reduced investment and in the emergence of slack in the economic system. Only as new markets are opened up and as new technology and new products are developed can the system expand again.

During the post-war period, exceptional economic demand made possible an exceptional upturn. It made possible a large increase in living standards for most of the people in the leading industrial nations. It invited expansionary government policies without setting off undue fears of inflation.

The period of unchallenged American supremacy was already ending in the 1960s. The initial challenge was felt in the automotive and electrical products industries. The West German economic takeoff was first visible in North America with the huge success of the Volkswagen Beetle. Later the Japanese would become the major threat, with their prodigious production of automobiles and electrical products.

The United States began to confront the problem faced earlier by other successful industrial nations. Newer equipment and superior organization of the productive process had undermined British industrial pre-eminence in the last decades of the nineteenth century. In the 1960s the same thing was happening to the United States. Markets for U.S. companies in key industrial sectors, both at home and abroad, began to erode.

The gigantic level of American military spending helped the other industrial countries in their catch-up effort. In the late

25

1960s, the huge expenditures on the Vietnam War directed funds away from industrial retooling just as the West German and Japanese threat was becoming serious.

By the end of the 1960s, the U.S. government faced difficult economic choices. The American merchandise trade surplus declined dramatically. At the same time, huge sums were flowing abroad to sustain the war effort. The result was that foreign central bankers were left holding a rising tide of American dollars. The process was exacerbated by the continuing flow of U.S. corporate dollars abroad in the form of direct investment in subsidiaries.

At the end of the 1960s the Nixon administration had a number of possible options for countering these mounting problems: it could cut back on military expenditures by winding down the Vietnam War; it could restrain the further flow of U.S. dollars abroad for investment; it could cut back on social programs paid for by Washington; or it could impose incomes controls on Americans.

For the most part, the Nixon administration did not want to make these choices. In one form or another, all of the choices would acknowledge that American dominance of the world economy could no longer be what it had been.

Instead, Washington decided to be all things to all people. It did not cut back on military expenditures; it did not rein in U.S. corporations abroad; and, generally, it did not impose restraint at home. The U.S. government resorted to the printing of extra dollars as a short-run expedient that would allow it to avoid making choices. The result was the generation of a serious inflationary spiral. While in 1960 consumer prices in the United States had increased by 1.6 per cent and in 1965 by 1.7 per cent, in 1969 they jumped 5.4 per cent and in 1970 by 5.9 per cent. (It is important to note that this new inflation began before the international oil price revolution of 1973, which would make it even worse.)

The new inflation at the beginning of the 1970s was a crucial shock to the international economic system. It signalled that all was not well and pointed to a shift in the international division of labour.

The inflation was quickly transmitted abroad, both because of the role of the American dollar as a reserve currency (a currency that could be used as a medium of exchange for all international transactions) and because foreign central bankers were holding vast and increasing sums of U.S. dollars.

The new inflation was caused by the unwillingness of the United States to deal with the implications of its relative decline.

It was not until August 15, 1971, that the Nixon administration let the world know that it recognized it had a problem. On that day, as good as any to date the end of the post-war era of clear American domination of the world economy, Washington took a number of unilateral steps. It ended the convertibility of the U.S. dollar into gold. This meant that foreigners (mostly central banks) holding U.S. dollars were holding mere paper, which could be exchanged only for other paper. The United States simultaneously embarked on an effort to improve the terms of trade for its products in the world. It established an emergency 10 per cent surcharge on the prices of all products entering the United States. It created a new tax measure, the Domestic International Sales Corporations (DISC), which allowed American companies to enjoy a very substantial tax write-off on products which they exported.

Armed with these weapons for restoring its competitive position, the United States negotiated a downward revaluation of the American dollar in relation to other currencies. This was to make it harder for foreigners to sell their products in the American market and easier for U.S. companies to export their production.

Because the United States was by far the largest economic unit in the non-Communist world, and because of its vast military and economic power, Washington was able to compel its trading partners to live with the new order of things. The flexing of American muscle was obvious for everyone to see. What was more difficult to appreciate was that Washington's actions were the result of U.S. decline.

Nor did these actions have the effect of halting that decline. In 1971, and again in 1972, the United States ended up with a merchandise trade deficit. The prodigious American productive machine could not even produce a surplus in its trade in commodities, an arena where American enterprise had been unchallenged for decades. In those two years, the United States ended up with a deficit in the current account section of its balance of payments.

The Oil Price Revolution

The new inflation was the first great shock to disrupt the functioning of the post-war economic system. A second inflationary shock came with the international oil price revolution of 1973.

Just as the United States set off the first shock, it was instrumental in generating the second one.[12]

During the post-war period, U.S. petroleum reserves fell steadily. By beginning of the 1970s, the decline could no longer be ignored. The traditional American policy of protecting most of its oil market for its own domestic production, in the context of low international oil prices, was no longer viable. The United States faced the prospect of sharply increased petroleum imports. Such imports would have the effect of worsening the American balance-of-payments problem, which, as we have seen, had already contributed to the crisis of 1971.

The role of the Organization of Petroleum Exporting Countries (OPEC) and of the major petroleum companies in the oil price revolution of 1973 was relatively straightforward. Both entities had much to gain from a sharply increased international petroleum price. Their role need not concern us here. The role of the U.S. government, however, does bear on the present discussion.

In 1972, and again in 1973, the U.S. government took steps to signal OPEC that it would not oppose a significant increase in the price of petroleum. Washington had a number of motives for giving the signal. It reasoned that a higher international petroleum price would spur the oil companies to explore for and develop the more costly remaining reserves in the United States, thus limiting the extent to which increases in imports would be needed. Higher prices would also lead to a reduction in petroleum use both by businesses and consumers, and would also lead, in the future, to reduced imports. Finally, the U.S. government believed that sharply increased international petroleum prices would hurt its major competitors, the Japanese and the Western Europeans, more than its own industry. This was because both the Japanese and the Western Europeans imported the vast bulk of their oil, while the United States still had major domestic reserves.

The oil price revolution went further than Washington wanted. In late 1973 and early 1974, OPEC quadrupled the international price of oil from about three dollars a barrel to about eleven dollars a barrel. Washington would have been happier with a price set in the six to seven-dollar range. Once launched, however, the oil price revolution proved very difficult to moderate.

The oil price revolution added fuel to the already raging fires of international inflation. The dismal era of stagflation had arrived. The era of unchallenged American domination of the world economy was ending.

The new inflation of the 1970s was, as we have seen, provoked by the consequences of American economic decline. The era of rebuilding the world economy based on the established industries was closing. A new competition existed among the major countries in the international economic system.

As the capacity to produce goods internationally came to exceed existing markets, the competition quickened. Each industrial country came under intense internal political pressure to maximize jobs at home. Unlike the old protectionism, which was based on tariffs, the new competition spawned an economic war of non-tariff barriers, measures taken by states to enhance industrial production at home. They took many forms: subsidies and tax breaks for domestic firms; customs delays designed to raise the price of imports; safety regulations for products that were actually disguised ways of restricting imports; domestic content requirements for the branch plants of multinational corporations; and many others.

The war of the non-tariff barriers was symptomatic of the most important economic event in the world in the past two decades: the emergence of advanced economies capable of challenging the supremacy of the United States. For Americans, used to thinking in the old ways that had become comfortable, or at least familiar, in the post-war years, this new world was difficult to understand. U.S. politicians had long trained the citizens of their country to think in terms of a bipolar world in which the Unted States and its allies were involved in a deadly military competition with the Soviet Union and its allies. In the real world of the 1970s and 1980s, American money spent on its arms race with the Soviet Union made it more difficult for the United States to deal with its new competitors—the West Germans, and especially the Japanese.

When Americans see television shots of Ronald Reagan and Mikhail Gorbachev together in Geneva, they are seeing a world they understand. What they find harder to understand is the strange, new world of economic competition with their allies, a world in which both the United States and the Soviet Union are declining in importance in the global economy. In the next chapter, we will look at how the United States is dealing with that new world.

Chapter Three

American Industry:
The Failure to Adapt

The increasing problems with the U.S. economy after 1970 had to do not only with the ending of the uniquely advantageous position of the United States in the world. The recovery of the devastated economies of Japan and West Germany was bound to occur sooner or later. It has become clear over the past decade and a half that the United States has serious problems in terms of its business culture, the way American business is managed, and the way American business understands its relationship with government and labour in the economy.

As it became ever more evident that something was wrong with American industry, it was natural enough for the spokespersons for American business to seize on their culturally inbred dislike for government to account for the problem. Business lobby organizations cited a myriad of reasons for the problems of U.S. industry: increased government regulation of industry in areas like pollution control; increased government spending as a proportion of the GNP; rising labour costs; and the skyrocketing price of energy (before 1982). Faced with competitive problems, American industry typically longed for the return of a simpler, more successful past in which government's role in the economy had been less significant, in which the U.S. economy was, quite simply, much more self-sufficient.

The trouble with their list of explanations for U.S. industrial difficulties was that their major competitors were doing better—despite the identical difficulties.

A celebrated article in the *Harvard Business Review* made this point:

> Although a host of readily named forces—government regulation, inflation, monetary policy, tax laws, labour costs and constraints, fear of a capital shortage, the price of imported oil—have taken their toll on American business, pressures of this sort affect the economic climate abroad just as they do here.
>
> A German executive, for example, will not be convinced by these explanations. Germany imports 95 per cent of its oil, we import 50 per cent, its government's share of gross domestic product is about 37 per cent, ours is about 30 per cent, and workers must be consulted on most major decisions. Yet Germany's rate of productivity growth has actually increased since 1970 and recently rose to more than four times ours.[13]

Could it be, then, that American business has experienced lessened profits and, therefore, a shortfall of capital to invest?

Economist Burton G. Malkiel has shown that for American business, the return on equity remained about the same during the years after 1970 as it had in the 1960s and that this was the case after adjusting for inflation.

But while this was true, investment in new equipment and in research and development as a proportion of the GNP declined significantly from the early 1960s.[14]

As Robert H. Hayes and William J. Abernathy argued in the *Harvard Business Review*:

> Expenditures on R and D by both business and government, as measured in constant, noninflated, dollars, also peaked in the mid-1960s—both in absolute terms and as a percentage of GNP. During the same period the expenditures on R and D by West Germany and Japan have been rising. More important, American spending on R and D as a percentage of sales in such critical research-intensive industries as machinery, professional and scientific instruments, chemicals, and aircraft had dropped by the mid-1970s to about half its level in the early 1960s.[15]

32

What was happening was that American business was becoming increasingly fixated on short-term return on investment (ROI) and was turning away from long-term, risky investments, which have been the key to real innovation. Short-term product imitation (to go after already established markets) instead of long-term creation of new kinds of products (with markets to come only later) was becoming the name of the game in American business.

Moreover, American enterprise was becoming horizontally integrated with the emergence of conglomerates that tied together totally unrelated businesses. As those at the top of the conglomerates were removed further and further from actual production, they concentrated on investment decisions that would result in short-term success. Careers were made and broken on the basis of the company's bottom line from quarter to quarter.

Executives changed firms with greater frequency as well, resulting in a strong disincentive for them to make long-term, risky investments. Success would be a long time coming. Moreover, in the short run, innovative investment is destructive of capital, because it makes obsolete a company's present stock of capital equipment.

American business executives were behaving more like bankers and accountants than like manufacturers. Over the past twenty-five years, the route to the top of American business has changed significantly. The proportion of those with technical, production-oriented backgrounds has fallen appreciably, while the proportion of those with legal and financial backgrounds has risen sharply. The number of top executives with "hands-on" production experience is much lower than it was several decades ago.[16]

The result has been that decisions surrounding productive investments have tended to be reduced to abstractions, based on the application of fashionable discounting techniques. Managers now make decisions by discounting estimated cash flows for a specific proposed investment. Once taxes and depreciation have been subtracted from expected cash flow, the rate of return for the investment can be calculated. If the expected rate of return is too low, the project is rejected.

While such methods were practised by only a minority of companies in the late 1950s, they have become virtually universal today. Discounting techniques tend to point companies in the direction of safe, short-term or imitative investment and away from long-term, innovative, and risky investment.

Economists Robert H. Hayes and David A. Garvin conclude:

> During the past ten years, the inflation-adjusted aftertax return on equity for U.S. corporations has roughly equalled its level in the 1950s. The ratio of shareholder dividends to total corporate operating cash flow, however, was 11 per cent higher in the late 1970s than in the late 1960s — and 30 per cent in 1980. The ratio of investment in new capital equipment to corporate cash flow, on the other hand, has generally declined since the 1950s. The problem is not that U.S. business lacks the money to spend; it is simply not spending the money in the same ways that it used to.[17]

This conclusion is significant. It indicates that private-sector managers of American business have been pursuing an investment strategy that has been undermining the long-term competitive strength of U.S. industry. Far from being the outcome of the rise of big government or the emergence of forces hostile to business, the woes of American industry flow from the decisions of private-sector managers themselves.

C. J. Grayson, president of the American Productivity Center, argues that for the past twenty years, American management has "coasted off the great R and D gains made during World War II, and constantly rewarded executives from the marketing, financial, and legal sides of the business while it ignored the production men."[18]

While a tougher world of increasing international competition was causing American business (which had previously had everything its own way) to become more cautious, it was teaching European and Japanese business how to compete effectively over the long term. It is important to appreciate just where these countries are coming from as competitors. The

Americans were coming out of the post-war experience of their own easy dominance. The Europeans and Japanese had been learning the hard way how to challenge that dominance. For the Americans, the habit of success made strenuous efforts for change appear unnecessary.

In fact, during the early years of the external challenge, American managers saw the option of massive capital investment to retool their productive plants as destructive of their existing facilities. In the auto industry, for example, it took a long time for the U.S. Big Three—General Motors, Ford, and Chrysler—to take seriously the challenge of offshore producers of small cars. Why, after all, should General Motors develop a small car and advertise it when such advertising would undermine the sales of the company's larger and more profitable products?

By the beginning of the 1970s, industrialists in many countries had learned the secrets of American success in mass production.

Historically, the strength of American enterprise had been its efficient mobilization of the factors of production and its exploitation of huge markets. U.S. management was unequalled in its capacity to stream labour, raw materials, and machinery into the productive process. It had learned the art of standardizing production and exercising precise control over every aspect of it.

In his book, *The Next American Frontier*, Robert Reich identifies three key factors underlying the historical success of American entrepreneurship: specialization by simplification; predetermined rules; and management information.[19]

Specialization by simplification referred to the breaking down of the steps involved in production into finite simple units. By identifying the mechanical movements required for production, enterprises were able to employ inexperienced and unskilled workers. Simplification of tasks made possible the efficient meshing of stages of production and use of machines by workers. It also made possible direct and effective supervision from above.

Predetermined rules allowed the simplified process of production to be monitored and controlled from above through a pyramidal management structure. The jobs of each level in the structure were carefully defined and tasks simplified so that top management knew exactly what was being done on each rung of the productive ladder.

Management information was the means by which those at the top collected the data necessary to apply the rules for the division of tasks, so that the simple steps of production could be most efficiently undertaken. Systems for collecting such information were crucial to the functioning of the whole.

The structure of American enterprise rested on dependable repetition. Its hierarchical structure and flow of orders allowed for precious little creative input from below. In fact, creative input from below was not valued. Taken together, American management techniques have been the legacy of what was called "scientific management," based on the ideas of Frederick Taylor. In summary, scientific management is not concerned with creative input from workers and is not concerned with the long-run well-being of the workforce. Instead, it is geared to getting as much out of employees as possible — in the short run.

Such an approach to labour, while it has been challenged by some advanced companies in the United States, remains substantially in place today. European and Japanese management systems, however, which involve serious input from workers and involvement of workers in significant decision-making, have been demonstrating their superiority, particularly in the past decade.

Business managers receive very different training in the United States and Japan. In the United States, while business managers are taught to be wizards of short-term financial manipulation, in Japan the emphasis is on working with people. South of Tokyo, near Mount Fuji, I visited the Kanrisha School, a veritable "boot camp" for business managers. The school divides the managers into small groups of eight to ten, each group led by a school instructor. From dawn to dusk, the managers are put through a gruelling program of chanting, reciting, singing, and physical exercise, including an all-night

40 km outing. To North Americans, watching the trainees is bizarre in the extreme. Through our eyes, it looks like the managers are being taught by rote. Actually what is happening is that their individualism, their sense of being special and apart from the workers they will supervise, is being broken down.

Visits to Japanese plants confirm that business managers there have an attitude very different from their American counterparts. When I met K. Tsukamoto, the Plant Manager of the Okamoto machine-tool plant north of Tokyo, I was surprised to find him dressed in the same blue-collar outfit as the workers on the plant floor. Mr. Tsukamoto has no office of his own. He works on the plant floor along with the office staff, also dressed in blue-collar outfits. The entire office and plant workforce occupy one vast room in the plant, so that workers who operate the machines can see the other workers who are responsible for making sure that materials for production arrive just when needed and that plant products are shipped to markets on schedule. (The plant produces for export to the United States and, increasingly, to China.)

At the Okamoto plant, graduate engineers work for up to three years on the machines before they are moved to jobs in design and management. Workers are free to go to the refreshment room when they feel the need for a break. On the whole the atmosphere is more relaxed and there is less of a sense of regimentation in the Okamoto plant than in North American plants I have visited. Workers and managers meet regularly to work out production problems. Ideas flow both ways in this industrial system.

(This Japanese example is not presented to prove that Japan is a nirvana of perfect peace between labour and management. There is a whole underside of cheap and exploited labour in the Japanese economy that is an important part of the picture. However, in the advanced industrial sectors, the Japanese productive system is formidable. Today, it is the American system which looks both old-fashioned and highly regimented.)

For decades, the American system of production was the

envy of the world. It had been ideally suited to the uniquely large national market to which it had been geared. Because it had mastered the art of mass production and economies of scale, American enterprise was well-adapted to extending its dominance over the U.S. market to foreign markets as well. The system peaked during the post-war decades.

Based on the principles of scientific management, the American economy and the economies of countries in the American sphere (including Canada) expanded more or less steadily during the post-war era. Those close to the centre of the system, Canadians among them, came to regard the features of the post-war era and the industrial system as normal. Its easy growth, its consensus about the goals of the economy, its shared prosperity—all these norms of the post-war era ended up being taken for granted.

In fact, the "economic truths" of the period between 1945 and 1970 proved to be both remarkable and transitory.

During the quarter century of American dominance, other nations were learning the secret of American production and were accumulating the means to duplicate it. By the early 1970s, the world capacity to produce the basic industrial products on which American mastery had been based—steel, autos, electrical products, machinery, and chemicals—far outstripped available markets. First the developed countries in Western Europe and Japan, and later the newly industrializing countries, such as South Korea, Taiwan, Singapore, and Brazil, mastered the techniques of American mass production.

As we noted in the last chapter, by the time the Nixon administration made its unilateral moves to change the rules of the international economic game, both the Western Europeans and the Japanese could challenge American competitiveness in the production of automobiles and electrical products. The growing invasion of the American market by imports in these industrial fields was testimony to this change.

At first the threat to U.S. supremacy involved the matching of U.S. capabilities by industries in other countries. Towards the end of the 1970s, the nature of the economic threat to the United States changed. The Japanese had successfully taken a

Import Shares of U.S. Market
(percentage)

	1960	1984
Auto	4.10	22.00
Steel	4.20	25.40
Apparel	1.80	30.00
Machine Tools	3.20	42.00

Mike Davis, "Reagonomics' Magical Mystery Tour," *New Left Review,* Winter 1985. Compiled from *Business Week,* the *New York Times,* and *Forbes.*

huge chunk of the American market for automobiles and electrical products. This represented the high point of the first kind of successful challenge to American supremacy.

The foreign challenge to the United States in key traditional industries can be seen from the accompanying table. The new challenge involved high technology and the specialized production of quality goods according to exacting specifications.

The High Technology Challenge

If new management techniques in the countries that compete with the United States are changing the human relationships in production, the other revolutionary change comes in the form of technology.

Many myths and much fear have surrounded the development of so-called high technology. High tech has spawned worshippers who pray to its creations in the hope that it will bring them salvation. Detractors live in terror of a mind-numbing world of high unemployment, with machines replacing people and with data banks storing the secrets of citizens and encouraging nightmarish official interference in people's lives.

So-called high technology refers to the newest labour-saving devices. The new devices, which centre on breakthroughs in microelectronics, have made possible the much more rapid accomplishment of many tasks. They open the way to the re-

volutionizing of industrial production, more efficient streaming and analyzing of information, and more efficient management of economic activities. In short, they are responsible for
the most important qualitative shift in the nature of industrial
organization since the rise of the automotive, electrical products, and chemical industries in the 1920s.

The essence of the industrial revolution over the past two
centuries has been the development of labour-saving devices.
Such devices have made possible an ever-increasing output per
unit of labour.

New labour-saving technology has regularly made particular skills obsolete and new ones crucial, and has led to the redefinition, displacement, and creation of jobs. Certain
technological advances have opened the way for whole new industries. The steam engine made railways and steamships possible, thereby allowing production and marketing of industrial
and agricultural goods in much larger markets. The internal
combustion engine led to the development of the automobile
industry and ultimately to the massive reshaping of the urban
environment. Both of these innovations, which served as key
engines of economic growth in their day, resulted in the development of labour-saving devices and techniques that reduced production costs. Modern steel-making, electrical
machinery, and assembly-line production, for example, made
possible the rise of the automotive industry.

Such changes have also wiped out certain kinds of jobs,
in some cases whole industries, and have contributed to shifts
in the balance of power among the industrial nations.

The list of victims of technological change has been a long
one. The skilled weavers of early nineteenth century England
were displaced by machines and were reduced from relative affluence to crushing poverty. Near Manchester, the weavers'
cottages are a reminder of the human price that was paid during the first industrial revolution. The families who lived in the
cottages, in some cases, had their incomes cut to one-tenth of
what they had been before the machines replaced the old
artisans.

The tragedy of the weavers has been repeated over and

over as technology has developed. Blacksmiths, railway firemen, and "hot-type" typesetters have all disappeared as the result of technological advance. Typically, the victims of change have not been those at the bottom of the economic ladder. They have been those whose skills have been made unnecessary as a result of new techniques of production and those whose jobs have been eliminated as a result of the disappearance of whole industries. Naturally, the victims have fought back, often with great courage, against their fate. In every case, however, the new techniques have triumphed and the old have given way.

Britain, the home of the first industrial revolution, declined when it failed to keep pace with innovations in steel-making, chemicals, machinery, and electrical products. By 1870 Britain had fallen behind Germany and the United States in these key sectors. Just as the rise of automotive production in the United States in the 1920s signalled an era of American industrial supremacy, so the emergence of the new microelectronic industries points to its passing.

Although the age of microelectronics is only beginning, its revolutionary nature is already clear. Microelectronic products have made possible enormous labour-saving potential in both the white- and blue-collar sectors of the economy. Moreover, microelectronics has itself become a new industry with vast growth potential. On the slopes of Mount Fuji, in Japan, there are now factories in which robots produce other robots, twenty-four hours a day, seven days a week. At night, the production proceeds in the dark with only a few booths lit up for technicians who oversee the awesome process.

Microelectronics enables much more efficient methods of research, correspondence, and writing. Computers simplify the preparing, revising, and reproducing of documents. Many secretarial functions are being streamlined and eliminated as a result. Computers have made possible a more efficient banking system, operating with fewer personnel. Many jobs, formerly done by researchers, can now be done much more quickly and completely by computers accessing data banks over the telephone. Huge quantities of information can be transmitted between computers in different centres without the use of paper and without paper being delivered from one location to another.

All of this has profound implications for employment in the white-collar sector of the economy. Moreover, the decentralizing potential of computers may ultimately have an effect on the design of cities just as dramatic as the effect of autos in the past.

Microelectronics is also significantly altering industrial production. Because it allows for information flows unequalled in the past, it makes possible the fine-tuning of the mobilization of the factors of production. This means that companies can save money by streaming materials into the production line at the moment they are needed and not before.

In manufacturing, microelectronics makes possible automated production on a scale previously unimagined. Welding robots on assembly lines have received widespread attention, but they are merely one eye-catching example of a much broader phenomenon. Over time microelectronics will revolutionize the assembly process in manufacturing, eliminating a large proportion of the jobs there. Jobs in manufacturing will shift to the production of components to be assembled and to the production of the high tech machinery that makes possible automated assembly of the final product.

Finally, microelectronics will shift the balance in the economy away from long-established industries to new ones. Work and life in industrial societies will be altered in ways we are only beginning to understand. It is easy for us, in retrospect, to understand the way the development of railways and then cars and then radio and television altered the way people lived their lives. Microelectronics reduces the movement of goods in favour of the movement of information. This shift will reduce the need for petroleum, for trucking, for highway upkeep, for paper, for mail delivery. It will allow people to relate to institutions from afar without travelling to and from centralized office complexes. This will affect the need for housing in relation to work-place, the need for rapid transit, and the organization of cities.

The high-tech challenge is one aspect of what Michael Piore and Charles Sabel describe as the shift from basic mass production to flexible systems production in the advanced economies.[20] Mass production concentrates on the manufacture of huge quantities of a small number of products. On the other hand, flexible systems production, utilizing the fine-tuning capabilities of microelectronics, concentrates on the output of goods according to much more exacting and varied specifications. For example, basic steel can be readily manufactured by labour forces in any industrialized country and in many newly industrializing countries. However, specialty steel, for aviation equipment and for certain kinds of machinery and construction material, demands much more exacting specifications. This type of production can only be undertaken by a much more highly trained work-force, in which the input of ideas from those involved in production is valued rather than discouraged.

Robert Reich argues that flexible systems production is alien to most of American enterprise and to the way that the U.S. economy is organized.[21] Flexible systems production, unlike that in basic industries, requires an enormous investment in human capital. Because employees frequently move from company to company in the United States, business does not like to invest large sums of money in the training of employees. After all, management reasons, what is the point of training an employee who will probably end up working for someone else.

The problem of trained personnel for flexible systems production goes far beyond the behaviour of the individual firm. It is a problem that is deeply embedded in the political and cultural ethic of American society. The difficulty of people moving often from firm to firm is an aspect of the high value American culture places on individualism and mobility.

Another aspect of the problem is the separation that exists, as Robert Reich shows, between economic and social policy in the United States.[22] American business culture, particularly in difficult economic times, emphasizes the need for hard-headed realism, for a concentration on the economic bottom line at the expense of what are seen as frills. These "frills" include education, training, and social programs to assist the people who are the victims of economic dislocation.

The American Response to the Economic Challenge

As we have seen, American economic decision-makers are faced today with a series of novel challenges. The days of U.S. supremacy in the production of basic industrial commodities are now long past. Furthermore, the transition to the new technology has been very problematic for American enterprise.

Despite the current faddishness of learning about things Japanese in the United States, the response to economic challenge from abroad has been ultraconservative.

This response has been manifested in a number of ways.

Because American workers cannot count on any protection for themselves if they must move from job to job as a result of dislocation, they and their unions have no choice but to dig in to protect the way things are currently done. The result is a very serious drag on the ability of American enterprise to remain competitive with that in Japan where lifetime job security exists for workers in a number of key sectors.

New product development, the training of workers for a new level of sophisticated production, the introduction of new technology—these things take a long time to lead to any payoff. In the short run, they are disruptive, expensive, and lead to an increase in costs instead of profits. For a manager who moves often from firm to firm, the payoff of such efforts may not be realized until he or she is long gone. Then the credit will go to someone else, while the original manager's record will have been one of higher costs and lower net income.

As we have already seen, American enterprise has increasingly developed a short-term approach to profit-making. In the past decade, much cunning and acumen have gone into corporate takeovers, and into the defence of companies against corporate takeovers.

"Merger mania," as it has been called, has become the consuming passion of American business management. In 1978 alone, eighty mergers took place in the United States involving companies with assets of at least $100 million. The following year nearly a hundred such mergers occurred. These amalgamations involved the transfer of assets of $20 billion from owner to owner. This was a far more interesting game for American managers to play than learning to compete with the Japanese and the Europeans in a world of ever-shrinking markets in relation to industrial capacity.

The inability to plan for the long term is the great disease of the individual American firm and of American society as a whole. It is analagous to the cretinous behaviour of British businessmen in the late nineteenth century, who insisted on putting their money into safe colonial ventures guaranteed by the state instead of investing in the upgrading of industrial productivity at home. The result for the British was decline vis-à-vis competitors. The result for the United States today is the same.

Because Americans have so much of their national culture invested in favour of unfettered free enterprise and against planning, they have become locked into divisive and short-run strategies for survival. Each industry, community, and group of workers has to fend for itself. Both the Japanese and the Western Europeans, with their very different approaches to business, government, and planning have opened up leads over the Americans in productive capability that will be very difficult to close.

MIT economist Lester Thurow, writing in the fall of 1985, concluded:

> There is a real danger... that America is falling from parity to inferiority if one examines comparative rates of growth of productivity. American productivity growth rates have been below those of Europe and Japan ever since the war, but more importantly they are still below those of Europe and Japan even though these countries have now essentially caught up. In the years from 1977 to 1983, productivity grew at the rate of 1.2 per cent per year in American manufacturing: one-half Germany's growth rate (2.5 per

45

cent), one-third the French rate (3.5 per cent), and less than one-third the Japanese rate (3.9 per cent). . . . And in the past 12 months (the second quarter of 1984 through the second quarter of 1985), there has been no productivity growth in the United States.

If such differences in growth rates continue to exist for very long, substantial inferiority cannot be far away.[23]

Finally, it must be said that in an era of U.S. economic decline, the dominant strain in American politics gives voice to a strident militarism. The militarism of the Reagan regime is not unrelated to American decline. In fact, Reaganism is, at bottom, an exaggerated, blustering, although unconscious, response to decline. Through the Reagan administration, Americans can tell each other that they will no longer suffer humiliation in the world. The Reagan administration has conveniently reinvented the notion of the bi-polar world of stark struggle between the United States and the Soviet Union. However perilous for mankind, this view of things involves reassurance for Americans about their place in the world. It does nothing, however, to solve the problem of American decline among the industrialized countries.

During Ronald Reagan's presidency, the United States has engaged in the highest level of concentrated foreign borrowing in history—so that foreign holdings in that country sky-rocketed from $576 billion in 1981 to $833 billion in 1984. Significantly, Canada was the second largest source of that foreign capital (next to Western Europe), at over $150 billion.[24]

By 1990, American net indebtedness is likely to reach $1 trillion. To illustrate the enormous shift that has taken place, consider this. By 1990, U.S. net foreign indebtedness could reach 16 per cent of the American GNP, while in 1967 the United States was a net creditor to the tune of 9 per cent of its GNP.[25]

Moreover, the level of American foreign borrowing has underlain another record-setting development—the soaring U.S. current account and trade deficits. In 1984, the U.S. trade deficit was $125 billion and the current account deficit (lower because of U.S. earnings on foreign investments) was $110 billion.[26] In 1985, the trade deficit reached $150 billion. U.S. foreign borrowing, the high American government deficit, and the highly valued American dollar combined to turn the United States into the world's greatest importing machine.

As a result, a new configuration in world trade emerged. All of the other major industrialized countries, including Canada, dramatically improved their trade balances with the United States.

As a survey done in 1984 by the staff of the International Monetary Fund concluded, "virtually all other industrial countries' external balances have improved during the past two years—Japan by $16 billion; the Federal Republic of Germany, Italy and the smaller industrial countries as a group by $8-12 billion each; and Canada by $5.5 billion."[27]

U.S. government and trade deficits have become the very dubious underpinning of the present American economic recovery. Moreover, they are a key, as well, to the economic recovery of all the other industrial countries. That is because all other industrial countries are now involved in a struggle for access to the American market. No country has bet more heavily on this option than Canada.

In a superficial way, the era of the "Reagan Restoration" has had some of the alluring features of the post-war era. The United States has resumed its role as the mainspring of the world economy, providing demand that now underlies much of the growth in the world economy. In the post-war decades, the United States played this kind of role. Then, however, things were much different. Then the United States was a net exporter of capital on a huge scale, while now it is becoming a net importer of capital. The United States enjoyed a perennial surplus in its trade in merchandise with the rest of the world. Two things prevented this productive superiority from simply running other economies into the ground—American investment abroad and U.S. global military spending. These latter two factors meant that the money the United States earned selling goods was reinvested in foreign countries along with additional funds as well. During the post-war decades, the United States usually ran a current account deficit, with the result that American dollars were flowing abroad into the coffers of foreign central banks.

During the post-war period, the United States played the role that Cambridge University economists have described as that of the "Big Spender." Through its foreign investments and military spending, it kept international demand high.[28]

This helped offset the naturally deflationary tendency that is built into the international trading system. The deflationary tendency exists because in international trade one country's surplus is another country's deficit. If a country runs a perennial current account deficit, it ultimately is forced to take steps to correct it. Two such steps are available (unless the country resorts to foreign exchange controls)—deliberate devaluation of the country's currency to make foreign goods more expensive as well as to improve the prospects for exports; and deflationary internal policies aimed at shrinking domestic demand for imports.

The world has seen both kinds of policies in the past twenty years. In 1971, when the Nixon administration in the United States sought a lower value American dollar, it was pursuing the first policy. Margaret Thatcher's policy of deflation at home keeps unemployment in the United Kingdom extremely high, but it also places limits on British imports and prevents a serious balance-of-payments problem for the United Kingdom.

Steps of these kinds to hold down imports ultimately provoke other countries to respond in kind, and this includes the countries that usually enjoy surpluses. It can thus be seen that the free market system of international trade has a deflationary bias.

Offsetting the deflationary bias has been the role of the international "Big Spender," a dominant country that pumps additional demand into the system and keeps it buoyant. Since 1982 the United States has resumed this role.

Salomon Brothers in New York estimated that 33 per cent of the growth in Canada's economy in 1984 was the direct result of exports to the United States (counting the indirect multiplier effects, the proportion would be much higher). The

48

proportion for Japan was 15.2 per cent, for West Germany 16.7 per cent, and for the United Kingdom 9.4 per cent.[29]

These export-led recoveries have forced industrialized countries to engage in an economic game that Cambridge University economist Ajit Singh has described as "competitive deflation."[30]

Competitive deflation is a system of cost-cutting to achieve international competitiveness—especially aimed at cutting government spending and labour costs. The system forces industrial countries to deny themselves the option of attempting internally generated economic expansion based on the use of traditional stimulative fiscal and monetary policies.

Since the "Reagan Revolution" began, the U.S. economy, as we have seen, has taken on the role of "locomotive" of the world economy once again. However, it has done so on the basis of unprecedented foreign borrowing and a dangerously high government deficit. The result has been a skyrocketing American trade deficit, a deficit that has led to widespread protectionist sentiment in the United States. That protectionism, as we shall see in the next chapter, is key to the free trade debate now going on in Canada.

Chapter Four

American Protectionism: The Stick

Canadian free traders do not merely try to tempt their compatriots into a bilateral deal with the United States through the use of the 8 per cent carrot, the lure of an increasing GNP—they also beat Canadians with a stick, warning them that rising American protectionism threatens Canada's access to the U.S. market. The reason the stick is so important is that the carrot is so unconvincing. To believe in the carrot, we have to accept the idea that access to the U.S. market is now sufficiently restricted for Canadian business, that there are would-be entrepreneurs in all parts of the country just waiting for the chance to get at that wider continental market. Once they get the chance, they will create thousands of new jobs in Canada, the argument goes. As we shall see, Canadian access to the U.S. market is already very wide, and therefore, it is implausible that insufficient access is a major factor in guiding the behaviour of Canadian business.

Moreover, since in our age people have become increasingly sceptical about experts who promise them the moon, by default, the stick—the negative argument—has become the crucial one in the arsenal of the free traders.

Their argument is as follows: Canadian exports to the United States are worth over $90 billion annually (in 1985) and yet we have no guaranteed access to the American market. Because the United States is now running record-high trade deficits, protectionism is on the increase south of the border.

Canada, the free traders argue, had better establish a free-trade area with the United States before Canadians get caught in the crossfire of a world trade war.

The free traders are very fond of warning that the status quo in Canada's trading relationship with the United States is not an option. We have to choose, they say, between free trade and the risk of a greatly reduced access to the American market.

It is important to examine Canadian exports to the United States and to assess the risks American protectionism poses to them. Are the risks substantial and would the establishment of a free trade area between Canada and the United States actually reduce them?

Before examining Canadian exports in detail, it helps to keep in mind that the institutional framework for a very large proportion of Canadian-American trade is provided by multinational corporations headquartered in the United States and operating on both sides of the border. Much of Canada's trade with the United States does not involve arm's-length transactions but deals within single companies. Figures from the U.S. Department of Commerce show that in 1982, American companies shipped $19.5 billion (U.S.) worth of products to their Canadian subsidiaries, while the Canadian subsidiaries shipped $21.4 billion worth to their U.S. parents.[31]

This is highly significant. It means that much of the Canadian-American trading relationship is not like trade between other countries. Characteristically, it consists of Canadians assembling products for sale in the U.S. market, producing parts for assembly in the United States, shipping fabricated resources and raw resources to the United States as inputs into the productive process, or selling fuel to U.S. industries and utilities. Because such trade facilitates the interaction between subsidiaries and head offices of multinational corporations, it is not resented politically in the same way that exports to the United States from abroad often are. In general, it helps to keep in mind that the role of multinationals in Canadian-American trade sharply reduces the risk of protectionist measures being taken to stop the flow of Canadian exports.

Let us now look at Canadian exports and make an assessment of which of our exports are vulnerable to U.S. protectionism and which are not. Discussions of this subject are often

Canadian Exports to the United States

Sector and Main Cdn. Origin

(billions of dollars)
Main U.S. Destination
(value of imports from Canada)

	1984	1983	1984
Live Animals	0.46	0.29	Minn., S. Dak., N. Dak.
Prairies	0.26		0.13
Meat and Fish	1.50		Conn., Mass., Rhode Is.
Atlantic	0.76		0.63
Total Food, Tobacco	3.00	2.6	New England, N.Y., N.J., Pa.
Ontario	1.00		1.41
Crude Materials	10.60	9.07	Minn., Dakotas, Ore., Wash., Alask.
Prairies	8.20		4.40
Wood and Paper	11.20		N.Y., N.J., Pa.
Quebec	3.40		2.40
Ontario	3.10		
Pacific	3.30		
Chemicals	3.50		Mich., Oh., Ill., Ind., Wisc.
Ontario	1.70		1.05
Prairies	1.20		
Iron and Steel	2.00		Mich., Oh.
Ontario	1.60		919.00
Non-ferrous Metals	4.90		N.J., N.Y., Pa.
Quebec	1.60		2.60
Ontario	2.90		
Tot. Fab. Material	27.70	22.80	N.Y., N.J., Pa., Mich., Oh.
Atlantic	1.40		12.10
Quebec	6.90		
Ontario	11.80		
Prairies	3.70		
Pacific	4.20		

Canadian Exports to the
United States (billions of dollars)
Sector and Main Cdn. Origin Main U.S. Destination
(value of imports from Canada)

	1984	1983	1984
Indust. Machinery	2.10		N.Y., N.J., Pa., Mich., Oh.
Ontario	1.60		0.77
Transport. Equip.	31.10		Mich., Ohio
Ontario	27.80		19.10
Tot. End Prods.	40.70	25.80	N.Y., N.J., Pa., Mich., Oh.
Quebec	4.50		28.30
Ontario	34.40		
Total Exports	82.80	66.30	N.Y., N.J., Pa., Mich., Oh.
Atlantic	2.90		44.30
Quebec	13.00		
Ontario	48.20		
Prairies	13.10		
Pacific	5.70		

Compiled from Statistics Canada, *Exports by Countries,* January-December 1984.

wrapped in vague jargon about "comparative advantage" and market opportunities. We get much further when we look at the specifics.

The accompanying tables summarize the key components of Canadian exports, the regions of Canada from which they come, and the most important regions of the United States to which they go.

When we examine the tables, we discover that Canadian exports to the United States depend very heavily on the sale of a relatively few key items to a highly concentrated regional market in the United States.

Let us briefly examine the riskiness of these exports in terms of potential backlash in the U.S. Congress. As can readily be seen, Canada's exports break down into a small number of familiar categories. The largest category is now transportation equipment, almost entirely autos and auto parts. This sector is already covered by an international treaty, the Canada-U.S. Auto Pact, and is therefore no more vulnerable to the whims of Congress than a comprehensive trade deal would be. The second category is fabricated materials, the traditional stronghold of Canadian exports to the United States. Here we are dealing with products that serve mainly as inputs into U.S. manufacturing. As can be seen from the table, these exports go to the major industrial states in the Midwest and mid-Atlantic Coast. American industry has been purchasing these inputs from Canada for decades and the threat to them from protectionism is small.

There are, however, some categories of fabricated materials where protectionist pressures have been felt by Canadian producers: steel and forest products. Because the American steel industry has been devastated by high imports, the U.S. government has exerted pressure on Canada to restrain exports from its steel producers, which are generally more efficient. While this has not threatened existing markets, it has limited the potential for growth in the U.S. market. Another area that has been subjected to protectionist pressures is the B.C. forest-products industry. Here the complaint comes from the competing American forest-products industry, centred in the Pacific Northwest. These producers have been hard-hit by B.C. competition, which has been increasingly effective as the Canadian dollar has fallen against the U.S. dollar. The specific attack has been on the low stumpage fees paid by B.C. producers who work the crown lands of the province. American producers claim that this form of competition from a system of land-holding in which the government owns the forests and leases them to private companies is unfair, as it involves hidden subsidies to B.C. producers. Considerable congressional attention has been paid to this grievance and there has been speculation that amendments could be attached to any comprehensive trade deal with Canada to force a settlement of this issue.

While these problem areas exist, they have not resulted in the American market being shut off to Canadian exports, even in the sectors about which grievances are felt. In general, Canadian exports of fabricated materials to the United States depend on their competitiveness in the American market. Historically, American corporations have relied heavily on Canadian inputs into their production, and this reliance has been strengthened through very considerable American direct investments in Canada in these fields. Such corporations are unlikely to turn on their Canadian suppliers in an outburst of protectionism.

This sector of the Canadian economy is an expression of the classic relationship between Canada and the United States, with Canadians selling industrial inputs and buying back the sophisticated manufactured products. Many doubts can be raised about how beneficial the relationship is for Canada, but people should not stay awake at night worrying that Americans are about to shut off the flow of these products from Canada.

The two sectors we have looked at, transportation equipment and fabricated materials, cover nearly three-quarters of Canadian exports to the United States.

The third major sector, crude materials, comprises totally unprocessed raw materials. Nearly 80 per cent of this category of exports (worth $10.6 billion) in all is made up of oil and natural gas. Far from being the target of American protectionists, petroleum exports from Canada have always been valued in the United States as secure, alternative sources to OPEC suppliers.

Once we include crude materials, seven-eighths of Canadian exports to the United States have been accounted for.

One other significant category (although small by comparison to the ones already discussed) is food and tobacco products, involving a total export of $3 billion in 1984. A subcategory, exports of fish and fish products from the Atlantic provinces, amounted to about $650 million in 1984. This is another area where a serious trade irritant exists between Canada and the United States. In January 1986, the United States put into place a countervailing duty on certain categories of fish exports from Nova Scotia on the grounds that fishermen from that province are subsidized by a broad range of social and economic programs funded by the Nova Scotia and federal governments.

This serious trade irritant casts into relief the problem with the whole idea of a comprehensive trade agreement with the United States. To satisfy this particular American objection would require the removal of virtually the whole system of transfer payments and equalization grants to the Atlantic provinces which is the chief underpinning of that region's economy. To grant the United States its desired "level playing field" in this case would involve a social revolution in the Atlantic provinces—not something to be lightly undertaken.

In addition to the irritant regarding the export of Nova Scotia fish, the United States has taken action detrimental to the export of Manitoba hogs. While the irritant is of importance to those farmers directly concerned, it is a very small matter in terms of Canadian exports as a whole.

While Canada does not export large amounts of grain to the United States, Canadian grain farmers may find themselves paying a price for an agricultural trade war between the United States and the European Community (EC). The Reagan administration has threatened retaliation against EC restrictions on U.S. grain exports.[32] If international grain prices are driven down in the process, Canadian farmers will be affected. Here, the irritant at issue is not to be found in Canadian-American trade but in the impact on Canadians of a trade dispute involving the United States and the EC.

When we survey the whole range of Canadian exports to the United States, we find that most exports face little or no threat from protectionism. While there are a number of areas where significant trade irritants do exist, and where actual or possible retaliation could occur, these areas are few in number and involve a very small proportion of total exports. Turning Canadian society inside out to solve these few cases where American protectionism could hurt Canadian producers does not make sense. Between major trading partners there are always irritants, which should be dealt with as such. But ongoing bilateral attempts to solve such relatively minor problems should not be confused with bilateral negotiations to put the entire trading relationship on a different footing.

It is difficult not to conclude that those who have waved

the flag of American protectionism to frighten Canadians into a comprehensive free trade deal have raised a largely bogus issue. Ironically, the irritants would not go away even with a free trade deal. U.S. representatives have made it very clear that they are not willing to remove the possible use of countervailing duties against what the United States sees as unfair trading practices of other countries even if Washington makes a free trade deal with such a country. Section 303 of the 1930 Tariff Act and Section 301 of the 1974 Trade Act authorize the U.S. government to impose countervailing duties on products deemed to have been subsidized by foreign governments and to retaliate against measures taken by foreign governments that harm American exports or enhance imports into the United States.[33]

Visiting Calgary in February 1986, William Merkin, the number two U.S. official in the bilateral talks with Canada, said there was virtually no chance the United States would give up the countervail. "That is as close as you are going to get to a non-starter," he commented.[34]

The countervail can still be used against Israel even following the 1984 free trade deal between Israel and the United States, and that would remain the case after a free trade deal between Ottawa and Washington. Israel fought hard for the removal of the countervail, and despite the fact that the country operates a formidable lobby in Washington, the countervail was kept in place. This is very significant because Israeli-American trade is tiny in comparison to Canadian-American trade, and Israel is one of the few countries in the world with which the United States has actually enjoyed a trade surplus in recent years. Perfect assurance of access to the American market for Canadian exporters would only come if Canada became a part of the United States—not a step many Canadians would want to take to solve a few trade irritants.

Oddly enough, the free traders first exaggerate the threat of American protectionism and then they underestimate it. As we have seen, the United States is very unlikely to give up the countervail—that is, to allow for complete Canadian access to the American market. On the other hand, the United States is also very unlikely to significantly limit imports from Canada. Canadian free traders forget that the reason Canadian exports are generally not threatened in the American market is because they have been built up through the institutional framework of an economy in which American multinational corporations have played a predominant role. It should be kept in mind that serious American protectionism has been developing not toward subsidiary economies like Canada's (which supply much-needed resources and fabricated products), but toward competitors like the Japanese who threaten to outgun the Americans in the key industrial sectors.

The difference between the way Canadian and Japanese exports are seen in the United States is very telling. While in 1985, Canada achieved a trade surplus with the United States of $20.4 billion, second only to that of Japan, this caused virtually no negative political reaction south of the border, while the Japanese trade surplus was a hot political issue.

Paula Stern, the chairperson of the International Trade Commission, the U.S. regulatory agency that deals with complaints regarding unfair competition from importers, has put the issue into perspective. Interviewed on Canadian-American trade irritants, she said: "This is an enormous trade flow and I expect it's not going to come without occasional frictions. You're going to hear complaints, but I don't believe they're disproportionate to the deficit."

Her perception that the Canadian-American trade relationship is not threatened with an undue number of irritants is borne out by the fact that since 1980, while there have been nine countervailing duty investigations into alleged subsidy practices by Canada, the International Trade Commission has upheld the complainant against Canada in only one case.[35]

Having now looked at the facts, let us look at the Canadian government rhetoric on the issue. In February 1986, External Affairs Minister Joe Clark undertook a speaking tour to promote the need for free trade. In a speech at Memorial University in St. John's, he warned that 300 protectionist bills were before the U.S. Congress, and that if they passed, $6 billion worth of Canadian exports would be threatened and 146,000 Canadian jobs could be lost.

Pounding home his message Clark said:

> Those are big, dramatic figures. This is a real threat. It's new and it's growing.
>
> That is the reason that we simply have to secure access to markets in the U.S. It is a question of securing what we have or there will be disruptions in jobs and in households across this country.
>
> The status quo won't work for Canada. That's clear.[36]

How does Mr. Clark's dramatic warning to Canadians stand up?

The argument that these "facts" underline the need for free trade is based on a chain of specious logic for the following reasons:

- Throughout 1985, while Progressive Conservative ministers warned about rising American protectionism, Canadian exports increased to the United States by $10 billion, from $84 billion to $94 billion. Far from Canada's access to the American market shrinking, it has been increasing rapidly. Moreover, as the U.S. dollar has fallen in value against other major currencies (not including Canada's) from its high point in the winter of 1985, the prospect has grown of an easing of the U.S. trade deficit which may take some of the heat out of the protectionist mood in Congress.
- If $6 billion out of $94 billion worth of exports is the total threatened portion of Canadian trade (as Mr. Clark's speech suggested), we are talking about less than one-fifteenth of the total or, to put it in a broader context, less than 2 per cent of the Canadian GNP. Does it make sense to turn Canada inside out to safeguard less than 2 per cent of the country's GNP?
- The chance that even a few of the 300 protectionist bills before the U.S. Congress will pass and be signed into law by the President is remote. Most bills before the U.S. Con-

gress are like private members' bills presented to the House of Commons in Canada. They are presented for the consumption of the people in a member's district or constituency. Estimating the threat to Canadian exports by totting up the hypothetical cost of these bills before Congress is as ridiculous as estimating Canada's government deficit by totalling up the possible cost to taxpayers of all the private members' bills presented in the Commons and adding that cost to the existing deficit.

Ironically, the way the Canadian government has dealt with the trade issue has actually had the effect of providing a focus for the protectionist sentiment in the United States that does exist against Canada. That became evident when the Reagan Administration managed to prevent the bid for trade talks with Canada on the so-called "fast track" from being blocked by the U.S. Senate Finance Committee by a single vote in April 1986. (The "fast track" method allows the Administration to negotiate with Canada and then submit the whole package to the Senate when the talks have been concluded. At that point the Senate can only pass or defeat the entire package, with no right of amendment.) The debate in the Finance Committee provided a forum for senators dissatisfied with the Administration's trade policies in general and unhappy with Canada over specific trade irritants, especially the dispute over the increasing export to the United States of softwood lumber.

As we have noted, the American system of government, based on checks and balances between the Congress and the Administration makes it very difficult for protectionist members of Congress to carry trade-blocking measures against the will of the Administration. However, what members of Congress can do with telling effect is to use the trade initiatives of the Administration to air their views on particular trade irritants.

The closeness of the vote in the committee meant the Reagan Administration would be under heavy pressure to make sure that the particular concerns of the senators were met.

During the debate in the committee, Senate Majority Leader Robert Dole drew up the following list of goals to be achieved by the United States in any deal with Canada:

- the elimination or reduction of Canadian tariffs, in line with U.S. tariffs on Canadian goods.
- a substantial reduction in Canadian government subsidies.
- improved access for U.S. exports of services.
- better patent protection for American products in Canada.
- increased access for U.S. firms to Canadian federal and provincial government contracts.
- a commitment by the provinces to abide by any trade deal.
- no exclusion for Canada from U.S. trade law (to keep the countervail as a potential weapon against Canada).
- an assurance that U.S. investors in Canada would be treated equally with domestic investors.[37]

In addition to these goals, committee members from the lumber producing states received assurances from the Administration that the softwood lumber issue would soon be settled in their favour, an assurance with serious implications for British Columbia's forest products industry.

Not surprisingly, Prime Minister Mulroney interpreted the close vote in the Senate Committee as evidence that he had been right all along about the threat to Canada from American protectionism and the need to negotiate a trade deal. In fact, it has been his government's insistence on negotiating a comprehensive agreement that has given the senators the chance to pressure Canada on a long list of items as the negotiations proceed. In the end, Brian Mulroney's public statements about the threat from American protectionism both strengthen the hand of U.S. negotiators in the trade talks and ensure that Canada will be forced to make most of the concessions.

The free traders have presented themselves as the bold advocates of progressive change, arguing that the nationalists are timidly hanging on to the old Canada of the past, unwilling to part with the status quo. In fact, the free traders are the heirs to those who have always wanted the most supine relationship with the United States. To them it is ironic that the nationalists fear the flight of the foreign-owned branch plants from the Canadian economy as a probable consequence of free trade.

Looked at in a broader perspective, we can see where the free traders fit in terms of the historic debate about Canada's options. In theory, Canada can have three kinds of relationships with the United States:

- An integrated continental economy with a wide-open door to American investment and no national policies which require American companies to invest in Canada to gain complete access to the Canadian market.
- A national economy in which access to the Canadian market for the sale of manufactured products is conceded in return for U.S. investment in Canada, and thereby the creation of jobs in Canada.
- A national economy in which Canadians strive to achieve a greater degree of domestic ownership and control of their economy so that trade between Canada and the United States (and other countries) is on the basis of greater equality.

Historically, Canadians have settled for the second option, the option of the branch-plant economy that was the result of the Macdonald National Policy. The free traders want us to fall back as a nation on the first option—complete continental integration—with no strings attached. It is true that while the nationalists have always wanted to move toward the third option, they have preferred the second option to the first.

Canada's Exports in a Changing Market

Even though Canadian exporters face few real threats from American protectionism, that is not the end of the matter. It is important as well for us to examine Canadian exports to consider their long-term viability in an era of rapidly changing markets.

Ontario is by far the most important province in terms of such exports. In 1984, that single province accounted for $48 billion worth of exports, or 58 per cent of national exports.

Moreover, well over half of Ontario's shipments to the United States, worth $27.8 billion, were in one sector—transportation equipment—overwhelmingly, assembled auto vehicles and auto parts.

Because the auto sector now constitutes the largest segment of Canadian exports to the United States and because it has been growing so rapidly in the 1980s, it deserves special attention. During the first half of the decade, shipments in this sector have moved from constituting less than one-fifth of the country's total exports to over one-third. During the period since the severe recession in 1981-82, auto exports have been the most important engine of economic recovery.

There are a number of reasons for this. U.S. economic recovery, fuelled by the very high government deficit, has depended on enormous consumer spending on durable items. Leading the way has been a gigantic upswing in purchases of automobiles. The increase in auto sales has been substantially aided by falling fuel prices, which have also had the effect of encouraging a shift in the market in favour of mid-size and large vehicles. Since the American auto producers have disproportionately located the assembly of mid-size and large vehicles in their Canadian plants, this country's industry has found itself in the right place at the right time. Not only have Canadian plants been turning out desirable products, their cost of production has been substantially aided by the falling value of the Canadian dollar against its U.S. counterpart.

Taking all of these factors together, it is clear that the huge increase in auto exports to the United States in the 1980s has resulted from fortuitous circumstances. The industry is a strong follower of the economic cycle, experiencing sharp downturns during recession, and strong upturns during good times. The reason for this is that the purchase of automobiles is something that can be put off during difficult economic periods. Consumer confidence and the highly fickle taste of consumers for particular models makes the performance of the industry a lot like a roller-coaster ride.

Under the Canada-U.S. Auto Pact, in place since 1965, Canada has seen periods of trade surplus and longer periods of deficit. The Auto Pact was a limited free trade agreement, a formal international treaty between Canada and the United States. Under it, companies could ship their products duty-free across the Canada-U.S. border, providing they met certain specified production minimums in Canada. These production minimums were the so-called safeguards in the pact. They were written into the agreement to meet the Canadian concern that the large auto manufacturers (General Motors, Ford, Chrysler, and American Motors) were all U.S.-owned companies with close relationships with American federal and state governments.

The safeguards were as follows: the dollar value of production in the Canadian auto industry would not be allowed to fall below its level in 1964; in addition (and far more important), as the Canadian market for cars and trucks grew, domestic production for cars was required to grow by at least 60 per cent of the dollar value of the growth in the case of cars, and 50 per cent in the case of trucks. The safeguards forced the auto industry to maintain a continuing commitment to production, and therefore, to investment and jobs in Canada.

A further word should be said about the structure of the auto industry in Canada. It is divided into two very unequal sections: the assembly and the parts industry. The assembly industry has been the strong component under the Auto Pact, always succeeding in running up large trade surpluses. On the other hand, the parts industry has been weak, with ever-growing deficits in trade. Putting the two sides of the auto sector together has sometimes resulted in trade surpluses, briefly at the beginning of the 1970s and again since 1982, but more often it has resulted in trade deficits for Canada.

To put Canada's auto exports into context, it helps to see the trade balance in the auto sector, along with the trade balance in other sectors. The accompanying table shows us those balances.

From this table, we see that while the auto sector has moved into a trade-surplus position overall (including Canada's trade with the United States and with Japan and western Europe), in the manufacturing sector as a whole there

Trade Balance by Geographic Region and Commodity Group
(billions of dollars)

By Country	Average 1973-1980	1981	1982	1983	1984
United States	1.10	3.70	11.30	14.10	19.90
United Kingdom	0.70	1.00	0.80	0.80	0.20
Other EEC	0.60	1.40	1.00	0.10	−1.40
Japan	1.00	0.30	1.00	0.30	0.10
Other OECD	0	0.40	−0.10	−0.40	−0.30
Other countries	−0.10	0.50	4.00	2.90	2.30
Total	3.30	7.30	17.80	17.70	20.80
By Commodity Group					
Agricultural Prods.	1.80	4.40	5.30	5.50	4.90
Crude Materials	3.50	3.00	6.20	7.20	9.60
Fabricated Prods.	8.40	16.70	16.00	16.30	18.90
Manufacturing	−11.00	−18.80	−11.00	−12.80	−15.50
Autos and Parts	−1.50	−2.30	2.20	2.70	3.70
Miscellaneous	0.60	2.00	1.30	1.40	3.00
Total	3.30	7.30	17.80	17.70	20.80

Compiled from Statistics Canada, *Exports by Countries,* January-December 1984.

remains a very large deficit. To be sure, that deficit has fallen dramatically as a proportion of the country's gross national product (GNP) since the beginning of the 1980s. However, considering the very high proportion of Canada's manufacturing exports accounted for by the auto industry, some cautionary words should be said about the future. As has been mentioned, one reason the auto industry has been so successful in the mid-1980s has been due to the fall in world oil prices. Steadily falling oil prices since the end of 1982, culminating in the dramatic collapse of prices in 1986, has restored to the global economy some of the features of the post-war era when low oil prices underlay the strength of traditional industries, in particular the auto industry.

It is not unlikely, however, that the period of low oil prices will be relatively shortlived. By the early 1990s, the current glut could be followed by a new shortage, with a new round of oil price increases similar to the ones that occurred in the 1970s. Certainly this is the strategy of Saudi Arabia, the dominant member of OPEC and the country with the world's largest petroleum reserves. By sharply increasing its production of oil in the winter of 1986, Saudi Arabia was driving high-cost producers out of the market, making their exploration and development costs uneconomic. Once OPEC's formerly high share of the world market has been regained, it is not unreasonable to expect sharp oil-price increases. If this prediction turns out to be true (and the highly volatile politics of the Middle East could, under certain circumstances, make it happen even sooner), the auto industry could face hard times in the 1990s, both in terms of the size of the market and in a renewed effort at downsizing and use of lighter materials.

These points are made because Canadians cannot afford to be complacent about continuing levels of very high demand for autos to sustain their exports and their economy in general. While enjoying the good times in auto production, Canadians should be planning right now how to make auto production a less central feature of their national economy.

If the rising importance of the auto sector as the engine of Canadian exports is reason for concern, the same can be said about the continuing reliance on raw resources and semi-fabricated products. While such exports are not in danger of disappearing, the long-run prognosis for Canada in such industries, in competition with producers in Third World countries, is not particularly favourable. Raw-material prices have suffered during the 1980s. Even more important, Canadian producers have found themselves being pushed up the cost curve in these industries in comparison to producers elsewhere.

While U.S. protectionism is not a major threat to Canadian exports, a real threat comes in the form of a changing global economy, in which Canada is over-specialized in fields that have highly volatile or even declining futures.

Chapter Five

Giving Up on an Industrial Strategy

In opting for a comprehensive free trade agreement with the United States, the Canadian government is making the judgement that this country should not pursue an industrial strategy. For a government that assumes that "a more market-driven economy" is the way to go, this is a judgement lightly made. For mainstream economists, it is also a judgement that is not troublesome.

However, for Canadians in general, the fact that free trade means the abandonment of an industrial strategy is the very heart of the question. Canadians have debated the idea of an industrial strategy, the setting of long-term goals for the economy through the co-operation of government, business, and labour, for at least a decade. The debate has been rather inconclusive and desultory to date, with the public mood and the key politicians sometimes swinging in favour of an industrial strategy, sometimes against. Ideologically, the Progressive Conservative government of Brian Mulroney is strongly opposed to an industrial strategy, believing instead that a move toward less government intervention in the economy will liberate Canadian business to generate growth.

If Canada signs a free trade pact with the United States, the government will not merely be indicating its position on the issue of government intervention in the economy, it will be determining that Canada can never have an industrial strategy. The reason this is so is that the price of admission to a free trade deal with the United States is the willingness to give up those instruments of economic policy which make an industrial policy possible.

We have already seen that the U.S. objective in a trade deal with Canada is to achieve a "level playing field" as far as the operation of American enterprise in Canada is concerned. Now let us see in greater detail just how the notion of a "level playing field" would affect the possibility of an industrial strategy. The American non-interventionist philosophy underlies the goals U.S. negotiators will pursue in their talks with Canada. An American "wish list" for the removal of Canadian non-tariff barriers[38] now looks something like this:

- An end to Buy Canadian programs by our governments. Canadian governments could no longer have a policy of awarding contracts which give domestic bidders an edge over American bidders. Since governments are the biggest spenders in society, abandoning the right to favour Canadian bidders means the loss of a major instrument of economic policy.

- Curtailing regional incentive programs to encourage the development of industries in economically disadvantaged areas, like the Maritime provinces. Such government money for industry would be banned on the grounds that it amounts to an unfair support for exporters. At stake here, as we have seen in the case of the American imposition of a countervailing duty on the export of Nova Scotia fish to the United States, are a wide range of provincial and federal government programs. Taken together, such programs form the most important base of the economy in the Atlantic provinces. At stake here are equalization payments, federal and provincial grants to industries in disadvantaged regions, and potentially Unemployment Insurance benefits paid to workers on a regular seasonal basis.

- The elimination of the Canadian production safeguards under the Canada-U.S. Auto Pact. Under the Pact, production safeguards require the big American auto producers to locate a substantial level of production in Canada. If the safeguards were eliminated, the Canadian government would have no course of action open to it should the U.S. auto manufacturers decide at some point to locate their future investments south of the border. The fate of thousands of jobs in Ontario's largest manufacturing industry would be entirely in the hands of the Big Three American auto producers. In trade talks with the United States, the Auto Pact safeguards are certain to be on the table.

- The banning of special pricing arrangements for primary products to encourage processing in Canada. Such measures have been used in the past to strengthen Canadian manufacturing based on the country's resources and have helped overcome the problem of the distance of our resource from large markets.

- Limiting marketing boards that restrict and control access to food markets across Canada. Canadian farmers could face unrestricted import competition from south of the border. Such competition could have very destructive effects, since climate makes Canadian farmers, although highly competitive by world standards, unable in many cases to be as productive as their American counterparts. Canada's External Affairs Minister, Joe Clark, has indicated that the Canadian government does not want to give up marketing boards, although he has been contradicted on this subject by other officials of the government.[39] But the issue will be on the table at the outset, and keeping marketing boards will almost certainly mean giving up something else.

- An agreement on investment to prevent future efforts at Canadianization of specific sectors of the economy. The Americans want U.S. companies to be able to operate in the Canadian market on the same basis as domestic firms. This is one of their biggest motivations in negotiating free trade with Canada. Such an investment deal would end the possibility of future programs like the now defunct National Energy Program (NEP), which was based on a system of differential grants to Canadian and foreign-owned companies. It would almost certainly also end the protection of special sectors of the economy for Canadian companies, the most important example being the banking industry and other services. It means that future Canadian governments will be powerless to take action to repatriate sectors of the economy.

- A breaching of the wall of Canadian cultural protectionism. In the fall of 1985 Canada's ambassador to Washington, Allan Gotlieb, reported to Ottawa in a confidential document that great pressure was being mounted by American corporations in opposition to Canada's policy of favouring increased Canadian ownership in the book publishing industry. Gotlieb warned Ottawa specifically that Gulf + Western Industries Inc., of New York, was threatening a "scorched earth response" if it was thwarted in completing its takeover of Prentice-Hall Canada Inc., a Toronto-based publishing company. U.S. officials strongly backed Gulf + Western and made it clear that they regarded the issue as a part of the free trade agenda. In the winter of 1986, Gulf + Western was allowed to proceed with the takeover of Prentice-Hall.

- An agreement formally linking the value of the Canadian dollar to the American dollar. Such an arrangement would be equivalent to the so-called "Snake," the system by which the currencies of countries in the European Community are allowed to float only in a limited range against each other. Such a deal would require Canada to pursue policies aimed at keeping its dollar in a narrow range vis-à-vis the American dollar.[40]

Canadian free traders will protest the inclusion of this item on the list, arguing that they oppose any such formal linking of the Canadian and American currencies. Despite their opposition to the notion of a currency agreement, it would not be surprising if American negotiators came up with such an idea. The reason for this is obvious enough: if the Canadian government can use deliberate devaluation of the Canadian dollar (easily achieved by lowering the Bank of Canada rate) as a way of creating an advantage for Canadian goods in the U.S. market while blocking American imports, Ottawa can effectively tilt a free trade deal in its direction. The Americans are unlikely to allow this to happen, if for no other reason than the fact that the devalued Canadian dollar has, in recent years, assisted Canada in running up record trade surpluses with the United States.

Despite the opposition of Canadian free traders to the notion of a currency link, the idea has surfaced already in serious U.S. political circles. Alexander Trowbridge, president of the National Association of Manufacturers (NAM), has called for efforts to keep the rates of exchange between the two currencies in line. The NAM feared that without such a currency link it would be too easy for Canadian exporters to help themselves to larger chunks of the American market, for example in the area of forest products. In addition to the NAM, Montana Senator Max Baucus has called for the inclusion of currency exchange rates in the talks.[41]

If a currency exchange agreement becomes a part of the American agenda and Canada accepts the idea, it would mean the end of the Canadian dollar as an independent currency with the effect that Canadian interest rates would be controlled in Washington.

As formidable a problem as what we might be asked to surrender is that Washington knows that the Canadian government regards a free trade deal and more foreign investment as virtually the only viable economic strategy for Canada. Because the Mulroney government has put all its eggs in one basket and has not even theoretically developed an alternative option, Canada's bargaining position will be very weak in the trade talks. Compounding this, of course, is the fact that Canada, at present, enjoys an annual trade surplus of over $20 billion with the United States. All this suggests that the United States will push hard to achieve its "wish list."

Politically, the American administration has nothing to lose if the talks break down since U.S. public opinion is scarcely aware that a free trade initiative is underway. In Canada, exactly the opposite is true. The Mulroney government has tied its fate to the talks. These very different political environments make the Canadian bargaining position weaker still.

The problem is that major concessions to make a deal possible would seriously undermine the powers of the Canadian federal and provincial governments to act in areas of economic policy. Conceding most of the U.S. "wish list," thereby giving up so-called non-tariff barriers, would mean abandoning the idea of an industrial strategy and thereby the potential for autonomous economic development.

How serious is it for Canada, if this country, once and for all, abandons the idea of an industrial strategy? To understand this, we need to consider a major development in the contemporary global economy.

Since the early 1970s, a strong contender has challenged the sway of American multinational corporations in the world economy. That strong contender is the concerted economic power of rival industrial systems throughout the developed world. It is now no exaggeration to speak of Japan Inc., Sweden Inc., West Germany Inc., or France Inc.

These rising national systems are based on a strategic working relationship between the states in these countries and leading corporations. This strategic relationship turns on long-range planning involving both the public and private sectors. What has been evolved are flexible systems which combine both long-range planning and plenty of initiative on the part of individual firms. The result has been the ability of these countries to target world-wide "market niches," where industries can be especially effective.

Several examples of market niches come to mind: the planned takeover of the world microchip market by the Japanese in the late 1970s; the development of the world's most successful high-speed, electrified train system in France (riding it in the summer of 1985, I was astonished to find myself two-thirds of the way from Paris to Geneva in 80 minutes); and the penetration of the world market for furniture, utilizing domestic resources, by Sweden.

Because the most outstanding examples of successful economic development have occurred in East Asia and especially in Japan, it is worth focussing on the experience there. The East Asian economic formula has been based on a singular combination of private initiative and public-sector planning. In Japan, the Ministry of International Trade and Industry (MITI) works with private-sector companies, unions, and citizens' groups to plan breakthroughs in targeted sunrise industries. Throughout Japan, dozens of consensus-making forums meet all the time. They represent business, labour, research scientists, and government. The role of government in such forums is to push for the consensus. Once a working agreement has been hammered out in such a forum, an agency like MITI works out specific details. But the success of the plan depends on all of the participants continuing to work together.

A good example of this approach is to be found in the robotics industry. Half the robots in the world are now located in Japan, where there is currently fierce competition among Japanese companies to dominate the market. Japan's worldwide lead in robotics did not stem from the working of the market system alone. Years ago, government, business, and labour targeted the production of robots as a key sunrise industry and made plans to encourage their use.

Government undertook research into the development of robots. Low-interest loans and attractive depreciation allowances were implemented to encourage companies to switch to the use of robots in their production facilities. In addition, MITI, robot manufacturers, and the Japan Development Bank sponsored a scheme to allow small companies to make use of robots. Such companies are normally not in a position to purchase expensive production robots. Under the scheme, companies like Mitsubishi operate showrooms in Tokyo where people from small businesses can come and check out robots, rent them, and make use of them in their factories. Visiting the Mitsubishi showroom in December 1985, I was impressed by how accessible the complex technology was to interested businesses.

The reason the developments in East Asia and in Western Europe are so significant is that a new economic model has been emerging in these national experiments. It was not so long ago that many analysts assumed that the future of the global economy lay with the continued expansion of multinational corporations, with such corporations operating on a supranational basis. It appeared that multinationals would be successful in breaking down the economic power of the nation state. If any state seemed to be powerful enough to take advantage of the rise of the multinationals to enhance its own power, it would have to be the American state, both because most of the multinationals were based in the United States, and because the United States has enjoyed a hegemonic supremacy in the world impossible for any other power. According to this view of things, U.S. multinationals were taming the world on behalf of an expanding American economic empire.

In the 1960s, this view of what was happening within world capitalism was commonplace. Now, however, such a view is very dated indeed. The American economic empire has been challenged successfully by a system of "national" multinationals based in developed countries where a close working relationship between business and government is in place. For people who have assumed that the central global socioeconomic struggle was between the American system of free enterprise on the one hand, and the Soviet system of command economy on the other, this development requires a large change of perspective. The developments of the last twenty years suggest that both superpowers in the world, the United States and the Soviet Union, have been experiencing economic decline vis-à-vis the new model of national capitalism that we have been discussing.

The model that has been successful (and there is a very wide range of national variations within it) involves, as we have seen, both competitive enterprise and long-range strategic planning, involving both the state and the private sector. This new model is not a compromise between the American and Soviet systems. Instead, it is the one model in the world which combines individual initiative with strategic planning and which allows for the creativity of the working population to be expressed and harnessed on a very wide scale. Neither the American nor the Soviet models do that. The United States is, as we have seen, tied to an economic model which emphasizes the short term over the long term and to a system of management which still emphasizes top-down con-

Growth of Productivity Per Cent	Average 1966-73	Average 1974-79	Average 1980-84
Japan	8.60	3.00	3.20
West Germany	4.10	3.00	1.70
France	4.80	3.00	1.70
United States	1.50	0.30	0.80
Canada	2.50	0.30	0.40

Department of Finance, Canada, *Economic Review*, April 1985, p. 174.

trol. The Soviet Union sets its economic goals through the workings of a massive, politically entrenched bureaucracy, in a manner which shuts the vast majority of its population out of any role in or enthusiasm for the productive process.

The new model that has emerged in East Asia and in parts of Western Europe is more in tune with both current technology and the needs of people in the work environment than any other system. Its triumphant emergence over the past two decades is no accident, and while no one can read the future, it is likely that this system will continue to gain in strength in coming decades.

Having described this development in terms of a new economic model, it should be emphasized that a wide range of possibilities exist within the model. The Swedish economy can be understood as a social democratic variant within the model, while Japan is a conservative variant. Within the model, there is room for fierce debates about the power of workers vis-à-vis their employers, and about the extent of the welfare state. What is important, though, is that a successful challenge employing common principles has been made both to the U.S. and Soviet ways of doing things.

To see concretely how the new model of national capitalism has successfully challenged the United States in particular, we need to look at the productivity gains enjoyed in the American economy and in other economies over the past two decades. The accompanying table illustrates how the United States has fared in productivity gains against major capitalist competitors. (Canada is included in the table as well to illustrate how our economy, with its strong American influences, has fared.)

Figures for productivity increase mean little if they vary slightly from year to year from country to country. However, if a consistent pattern emerges in which some economies outperform others on this score, this is a matter of real significance. For two decades Japan, West Germany, and France have consistently enjoyed productivity increases substantially higher than those in the United States and Canada. It is this long-term process which is making the United States, and Canada along with it, less and less competitive in global economic terms. Only those who fail to see reality can watch such productivity figures year after year without wondering whether the economic model operating in the United States, and copied in Canada, is not now second-best.

The result of U.S. failure to keep pace with competitors within the developed world (not to mention problems with the newly industrializing countries) has been an emerging debate within the United States on how to deal with America's problem of lack of competitiveness.

Two broad positions have emerged in the U.S. debate: they can be labelled protectionist and internationalist. The protectionists include those in Congress who are pushing for legislation that will impede imports of various products into the United States. But the protectionists also include the wing of the Reagan administration which favours a strategy of negotiating bilateral trade deals with particular countries. This wing of the administration falsely labels itself as pro-free-trade. In fact, its position involves the United States turning away from the multilateral trading system in favour of bilateral agreements. The purpose of this strategy is both to bludgeon America's most serious trading competitors (the Japanese head this list) into concessions and to define a new international economic sphere in which U.S. power can be confident of supremacy. In effect, this wing of the administration is willing to redefine that area of the world within which the United States can enjoy hegemony. At the end of World War II, American strategic thinkers defined this area, the so-called

"Grand Area," to include, at a minimum, the western hemisphere, western Europe, and Japan. The new strategy of bilateral trade deals involves a tacit move toward a redefinition of the "Grand Area" in recognition of America's competitive problems.

The redefinition of a viable external economic sphere is not a new event in the history of great powers. At the end of the nineteenth century, Britain, the country that had launched the first industrial revolution, was forced to narrow its economic orbit substantially in the face of competition from the other industrializing powers.

There remains, however, a powerful wing of American political and business opinion in favour of maintaining the full international economic system as evolved in the post-World-War-II period. A comprehensive trade agreement with Canada would therefore mean a victory for the protectionist wing of the Reagan administration that advocates this redefinition of a new world economic sphere.

Economists have been advising Canadian governments to sign a free trade deal with the United States for decades. The difference is that now the advice is being heeded because it fits well with the neo-conservative economic preferences of the Mulroney government. Ironically, the acceptance of that advice coincides with a development in the world economy which goes a very long way to invalidating the assumptions of neo-classical economists. It has to do with the emergence of East Asia, particularly Japan, as an economic power to be reckoned with.[42]

Unquestionably the rise of East Asian capitalism as a successful challenger to the United States has been a crucial factor in setting the stage for a bilateral trade deal between Canada and the United States. After all, it has been the rise of East Asia more than anything else that has led to the growing American trade crisis. And it has been the rising U.S. trade deficit that has spurred the protectionist movement that has caused Canadian economists and the Canadian government to favour a deal.

When we look a little deeper into the trade crisis between

East Asia and the United States, we see the irony. East Asian economies, especially that of Japan, as we have seen, have been organized around a singular combination of private initiative and public planning and support. The East Asian economic miracle has decidedly not been based on the individualistic model of competitive economy favoured in the United States. Rather, it has been based on the synergy between public and private sectors which takes advantage both of long-term strategic planning and of competition.

As we have already seen, to achieve a trade deal with Washington will require Canada to give up the major tools advanced countries use to pursue industrial strategies. We will willy-nilly be left with nothing but the American "level playing field," the competitive American economy in which the state plays no creative role. We will be adopting the American model just when its weaknesses are becoming most evident.

Even more ironic, we will be adopting the American model in spite of the fact that our own economic history in Canada gives us a model far closer to the one that has been emerging elsewhere in the industrialized world, not only in East Asia but in Europe as well. This is not to claim that Canadian economic performance has been any kind of miracle. It is to claim, however, that Canada's own economic history has been characterized by an interaction between the public and private sectors whose principles are worth preserving. We do need an alternative to the status quo in Canada; on this point the Macdonald Commission was right. We would do better, however, to examine the successes of other industrial economies and our own history than to go over to complete economic integration with the United States, on the basis of the American economic model.

Chapter Six

Canada's Real Economic Problems

As a result of the government's free trade initiative, the severe underlying problems of the Canadian economy are not receiving the attention they deserve. By focussing on those problems, we can shed further light on whether free trade makes sense for Canada and also examine alternatives to free trade.

The best clue to the underlying problems of the Canadian economy comes from the figures for Canada's balance of payments (current account). Two totals make up the current account: merchandise trade; and trade in invisibles. The merchandise trade balance is reached by subtracting the dollar value of the country's exports from the value of its imports. The trade in invisibles is reached by doing the same with the country's foreign balance in dividend and interest payments and in tourism. Then, the overall current account is calculated by putting the merchandise and invisibles accounts together. The accompanying table charts the behaviour of the country's current account.

Current Account Balance   billions of dollars

	Average 1971-1980	1981	1982	1983	1984
Balance of Trade	3.00	7.30	17.80	17.70	20.80
Balance on Services	−6.10	−14.90	−16.50	−16.80	−19.70
Balance on Goods and Services	−3.00	−7.60	1.30	0.90	1.20
Net Transfers	0.50	1.50	1.40	0.80	0.80
Balance on Current Account	−2.50	−5.80	2.70	1.70	2.00

Statistics Canada, *Economic Review,* April 1985.

Perennially, Canada has had a large surplus in its merchandise trade account and a large deficit in its invisibles account. For most of the past decade, this has resulted in an overall current account deficit. In 1981, Canada's current account deficit peaked at $5.7 billion. Then came the severe recession and the subsequent recovery. The recession led to a very sharp reduction in Canada's imports and the recovery was based on a growing, indeed spectacular, performance in exports. Although the deficit in invisibles remained very high, the strong export performance moved the current account balance into surplus—temporarily. In 1985, despite a $19 billion merchandise trade surplus, the deficit in invisibles stood at over $20 billion and therefore the current account was negative to the tune of $1.5 billion.[43]

What this means is that even very high merchandise trade surpluses can only keep the country close to balance in its current account. Anything less will result in the balance of payments becoming sharply negative.

Why is Canada's performance in invisibles so weak? Part of the explanation lies with the country's customary deficit in tourism—in 1984, Canadians spent $2.2 billion more abroad than foreign visitors spent in Canada.[44] But the tourism account only amounts to about 10 per cent of the deficit. The rest is made up of Canada's international transactions in dividend and interest payments. The cause of the problem is quite simple: the enormous level of foreign investment in Canada has led to a huge and growing annual outflow of funds in the form of interest payments and dividends. Dividends are paid to the shareholders of foreign-owned subsidiaries. Interest payments are made to foreign institutions which have loaned money to Canadian public or private-sector companies and governments. It is interest payments to non-residents that make up the largest portion of the deficit on services. In 1984, Canada's deficit on net interest payments reached a colossal $9.4 billion.[45] Figures from the U.S. Department of Commerce show that in 1982, U.S. investments in Canada totalled a staggering $110 billion and that 914,000 Canadians worked for American-owned enterprises.[46]

82

What Canadians often forget is that foreign investment equals foreign debt. External investors do not put their money here for free. They expect to earn a return on it.

Ironies abound on the subject of foreign indebtedness and its consequences. Now, as we have seen, the United States has become a net debtor nation for the first time since the end of World War I. The American foreign debt (which results, as does the Canadian, from foreign investment) is growing prodigiously. The United States may be a net debtor to the tune of $1 trillion by 1990. American commentators are growing alarmed at what this will do to the U.S. standard of living as Americans have to work to make payments to foreigners.

In the United States, no serious commentator argues that having a high and growing net foreign debt is beneficial. American commentators have several concerns with the foreign debt:

- They realize that paying interest on it will necessitate cutting into the American standard of living in favour of foreigners.
- They fear the loss of independence that follows from the need to pursue policies to keep foreign money in the United States.
- They worry that the United States may have to maintain high real interest rates in comparison with other countries to prevent foreign investors from moving their funds elsewhere. High real interest rates, of course, tend to inhibit long-term investments in basic industries. As Lester Thurow wrote: "...high real interest rates discourage the economy from making the long-term investments it ultimately needs to be competitive."[47]

All of these concerns reflect the fact that American analysts do not believe it beneficial for their country to be the recipient of a large net level of foreign investment.

Even if the U.S. net foreign debt reaches $1 trillion, it will still be substantially lower than the Canadian foreign debt, on a per capita basis. In contrast, it is a leading policy of the

Canadian government to increase our foreign debt just as rapidly as possible.

Along with its quest for free trade, the critical policy of the Mulroney government has been to seek an inflow of foreign capital. To further this policy, the government has junked the Foreign Investment Review Agency (FIRA), replacing it with Investment Canada; it has scrapped the National Energy Program (NEP); and it has initiated what amount to virtual giveaways of crown corporations in the aircraft industry—beginning with the sale of DeHavilland to Boeing, to be followed by the sale of Canadair.

Canada's quest for U.S. investment indicates that the Mulroney government sees no alternative to the policy of continuing to tie the Canadian to the U.S. economy, not only in terms of merchandise trade, but also in terms of the sourcing of new technology, the importation of industrial machinery, and parts and components for production—and perhaps most important, in terms of techniques of industrial management.

Even though Canada's branch-plant economy is rapidly being altered as the freer trade measures agreed to in the last round of GATT talks are implemented, the institutional arrangements that tie Canadian subsidiaries to their parent companies remain of vital importance, and it needs to be understood that the Mulroney government is continuing to tie Canada to a declining industrial economy, an economy whose policies (as we have seen) leave it no longer at the cutting edge of industrial technique.

Chapter Seven

The West and Free Trade

Central Canadian domination of the economy over the past century has made it very difficult for Canadians to agree on a common economic policy. Western regionalism was the inevitable response to the federal government's historic plan for the West at the time of Confederation—to make use of it as a colony for central Canada.

The prairies were essential to John A. Macdonald's economic strategy. Across them the national railway to the Pacific was to be built. That railway would tie the new Dominion together, ensuring British Columbia's entry into Confederation. It would serve as an Imperial route linking the Atlantic and Pacific. Not least, it would provide an enterprise that would enrich the bankers and railway entrepreneurs of the East. Finally, at some point in the future, it would provide a route to ship the products of the prairies to market. This final ambition, whose fulfillment would ultimately be of the greatest importance in tying the economy of the country together, was little more than a hope and a prayer when the railway was being built. It was not until the 1890s, after the Canadian Pacific Railway was completed, that a strain of wheat was developed that could flourish in the short, dry summers of the prairies.

By the turn of the century, though, wheat was fast becoming the country's most important export. Prairie wheat was shipped to market by rail to the Lakehead at Port Arthur and from there by freighter to Montreal and beyond to Europe. (Later, with the building of the Panama Canal, wheat would also be shipped to Vancouver in large quantities, and from there overseas.)

It was western Canadian wheat that gave the national economy its dynamism in the key first decade of this century. Wheat exports drew foreign currency into Canada and allowed Canadians to buy the goods of other countries. Wheat farmers bought machinery and other manufactured products from eastern Canada. The federal government sponsored large-scale immigration to the prairies from Europe and the United States.

But as their importance to the national economy grew in the early twentieth century, so too did the resentment of western farmers in opposition to their inequitable place in it. The National Policy, as the Macdonald economic strategy was called, was ordered to make the West a hinterland to service the manufacturers, bankers, and railwaymen of central Canada.

The centre of this evil system, as western farmers saw it, was the tariff. The tariff forced the West to buy the manufactured goods of the East, paying more for them than they would have to have paid had they been able to import from abroad.

This sentiment was expressed in 1910 by J. W. Scallion, the honorary president of the Manitoba Grain Growers' Association when he said:

> The prices of the produce of the farm are fixed in the markets of the world by supply and demand and free competition when these products are exported, and the export price fixes the price for home consumption. The supplies for the farm are purchased in a restricted market where the prices are fixed by combinations of manufacturers and other business interests operating under the shelter of a protective tariff...
>
> [Nothing] would meet with greater favour or stronger support from the farmers of western Canada than a wide

measure of reciprocal trade with the United States.[48]

As Gordon Laxer has written:

Historically, western Canadian farmers were vigorous advocates of free trade and for good reason. . . . Protection for special eastern interests became one of western Canada's main grievances within Confederation. Support for free trade became synonymous with western Canada's political identity. To oppose free trade—especially in Alberta and Saskatchewan—was tantamount to 'treason' or being beholden to eastern interests.[49]

The historic opposition of western farmers to the tariff has created a mind-set throughout the region in favour of free trade. Successive populist political movements spawned in the prairies have fought for free trade. Some of the country's most inspired political leadership has come in the good fight against the tariff.

Today, though, the farmers' organizations have rethought the issue, and now oppose a comprehensive trade deal with the United States.

Why have farm associations changed their position? The reason is quite simple. As we have already seen, free trade is no longer primarily a question of tariffs. By 1987, as the full effects of the latest GATT tariff cuts take effect, most U.S. products will enter Canada duty-free. Sixty five per cent of American industrial imports will face no tariff, while a further 25 per cent will encounter a nominal duty of 5 per cent or less. In addition, Canada has long had sectoral free trade in agricultural machinery with the United States. When all these things are considered, it is apparent that the historic grievance of the west—that eastern interests are sheltering behind the tariff—is now substantially untrue. And yet, despite the contemporary position of farm organizations, the historic sentiment in the region for free trade lingers.

Today the real issue for the west, as for the rest of Canada, is non-tariff barriers. How will the interests of western Canada fare in a trade deal whose primary purpose is their elimination?

In terms of non-tariff barriers, a number of threats are posed to the west. There is already a controversy about agricultural marketing boards and whether they will be bargained away as restraints in negotiations with the United States.[50] In addition to marketing boards for farms, there is the issue of whether two-price systems for resources such as petroleum would be permissible under a free trade arrangement with the United States. Two-price systems in petroleum have been important in allowing the establishment of a major petrochemical industry in Alberta. Bargaining away the right to operate a two-price system could mean the shifting of a large part of that industry closer to the centre of the continental market. Finally, there is the broader issue of industrial strategy. Through the Alberta Heritage Fund and other similar provincial and federal funding sources, money is pumped into industrial and transportation development in the West. Will such investment be defined as export subsidies and limited in the future with serious consequences for the economic future of the West?

It is these non-tariff issues which are central to the West today. That this is the case is highlighted, when we examine the potential impact of free trade on Canadian agriculture. American officials have made it clear that they will insist on including agriculture in the bilateral trade talks with Canada. The inclusion of agriculture in the negotiations will open a series of difficult problems for Canadians.

Despite its reputation as a free market economy, the United States practises considerable protection with respect to agriculture. Since the 1920s, when American agriculture was suffering as a result of low prices and poor markets, a broad-based system of supports for U.S. agriculture has been put into place.

In Canada, supports tend to be aimed more narrowly at specific agricultural sub-sectors. Some of the most important supports include: freight-rate subsidies to grain farmers for the movement of their product to port (the replacement for the old Crow Rate); the use of the Canada Wheat Board as the sole marketer for Canadian grain; cash subsidies for hog farmers; and restrictions on entry into the Canadian market for poultry and dairy products in favour of local producers.

These kinds of support systems for Canadian farmers are seen with disfavour in the United States. American negotiators are likely to insist on the removal of some or all of these systems of support, while they maintain that the U.S. systems should remain in place because they are not targeted so directly at specific sectors.

Free trade with the United States is likely to lead to an immense shake-up of Canadian agriculture, threatening whole sectors with severe new competition from south of the border. In the process, already hard-pressed farm communities in Canada will be subjected to greater strains than ever.

Chapter Eight

The Canadian Way of Life

Canadians have often been told that the stakes in the debate about free trade with the United States are purely economic, that the issue is whether a sound business deal can be had. There is evidence, however, that what will be on the table in the trade negotiations is no less than a series of key decisions about our way of life, the values of our society, the character of our communities. What is involved is "culture," not in the narrow sense of specific institutions and their products, but in the broad sense of the world view of our society.

For some people, concern about the impact of a trade deal on culture is a red herring, used to lure Canadians off the path of making a sound economic decision. One of the people who feels this way is Simon Reisman, Canada's chief trade negotiator. In the spring of 1985, before the Prime Minister picked him to head the Canadian negotiating team, Reisman said in a speech to the Ontario Economic Council that he could not understand why some people made so much fuss about the protection of Canadian culture.

He confessed himself unable "to find convincing evidence" that any threat to Canadian culture could be a by-product of full free trade with the United States.[51]

Another supporter of free trade who dismisses the concern about culture in a particularly frank way is Anthony Westell, Associate Dean of Arts at Carleton University. He believes, quite simply, that there is no problem because there is no

Canadian way of life. In December 1984, in a lengthy article in the journal *Perspectives*, Mr. Westell contended that it "is misleading in modern circumstances to think of national cultures."

"To be a Canadian," he contended, "does not signify a way of life, or a set of values beyond attachment to the community and loyalty to the national state. So the fear that closer association with the United States will erode a Canadian identity in the making or abort a Canadian culture about to be born is unfounded."[52]

Are there values, ways of living, that divide Canadians from Americans, and if so, will those values be on the table in the trade talks? To make sense of this, we have to get past the obvious impact of American popular culture on societies all over the world. Huge portraits of American movie idols in Paris, and giant renderings of the Flintstones on the walls of buildings in Tokyo were two examples of that influence that struck me during my travels in recent months. But, beneath this surface sameness, are there enduring and important differences between societies that matter to their inhabitants?

I believe there are such differences between Canada and the United States, and that they are tangible, important to the way Canadians live, and that they are at stake in the trade talks.

Four areas come to mind:

- Violence in the two countries
- The tone and design of Canadian and American cities
- Attitudes to social programs
- The importance of the military in the two countries

Violence is important to the way a society lives, because it places limits on the sense of safety citizens have in going about their everyday activities. It is all well and good to talk about the common culture of North America, but if it turns out that one country is immensely more violent than the other, then perhaps it is the similarities that are superficial and the differences that are profound. American sociologist Seymour M. Lipset, a long-time observer of the two countries, has made the point that there is a sharply lower level of violence in Canada compared to the United States.

The United States is wracked with violence on a scale unique in the developed world. In the spring of 1985, a report by twelve prominent university experts for the Eisenhower Foundation concluded that the "level of crime in the United States remains astronomical when compared with that of other industrialized democracies."[53]

In Atlanta, Georgia, where medical epidemics have long been studied, the Violence Epidemiology Branch now analyzes the American problem with violence.[54] There are nearly twenty thousand murders a year in the United States, compared with about six hundred per year in Canada. On a per capita basis, while there are about 2.5 murders per hundred thousand people per year in Canada, in the United States the rate runs at 8.3 per hundred thousand.[55]

In many large American cities, the murder rate is much higher. In New York, it runs at 23 per hundred thousand, in Philadelphia at 18—and in Detroit at an astronomical 49, twenty times the Canadian rate. To put Detroit's murders in perspective, at that rate Metropolitan Toronto would have over 1000 murders a year, instead of the 57 it actually had in 1985.

Of course, all industrial societies have their violence and their mass murderers, including British Columbia's Clifford Olson. The difference is one of scale. In the United States the problem of violence is epidemic in comparison to other industrial countries. In the past year I felt quite comfortable exploring Tokyo, Paris, and Stockholm at night, but not New York, Washington, and Chicago, although presumably as a Canadian I have much more in common with people in the American cities.

Feeling more at home in Canadian, Japanese, and European cities than in American cities has to do not only with the fear of violence but with the design and shape of American cities in comparison to those in other industrial nations. The design of American cities reflects much wider values that get at the very core of the American "way of life."

The typical American city is, as Toronto historian William

Kilbourn describes it, "a doughnut"—it is made up of rings of affluence around a ruined, often empty, shell at the centre. Detroit, Philadelphia, Chicago, and countless smaller American cities share this pattern of wealthy suburbs surrounding frightening, desolate city centres. Even New York, often cited as a major exception, is much more like this than are the great cities of Europe, Japan—and Canada. Metropolitan Toronto, a city of three million, works—much to the astonishment of many Americans—because it has not died at the centre.

The reasons American cities have taken the shape of the doughnut are not hard to find. In the American quest for individual freedom, the flight to the suburbs, away from the need to pay taxes to keep up the core of a city, has reawakened the ancient spirit of the frontier in Americans. The result is decaying city centres inhabited by those whom the larger white, middle-class society has rejected.

If the American emphasis on individual mobility has had its impact on the shape of U.S. cities, it has also had its effect on social programs across the border. The idea of providing a government-operated safety net on behalf of the sick, the old, the disadvantaged, and the unemployed is a much more controversial one in the United States than in Canada. While in Canada state-supported universal medicare is something that no political party dares to attack, in the United States, universal medicare does not exist and it is routine for the White House to propose cuts to the meagre government spending for medical services for the poor now in place (as it did in preparing its 1987 budget proposals).

While government payments for social programs are widely supported in Canada, they are increasingly under attack in the United States. While in Ottawa, the government retreated from plans to de-index old-age pensions, in Washington conservative authors like Charles Murray, who want to scrap all federal involvement in social programs, are very popular with the White House. In his book, *Losing Ground*, economist Charles Murray, Senior Research Fellow at the Manhattan Institute for Policy Research, warned against the rise of a culture of dependency due to welfare spending by

94

the U.S. government. He linked welfare payments to the prodigious rise in illegitimate births in the United States and advocated the complete elimination of all federal government programs directed at the poor.

One of the reasons that social programs receive wider support in Canada than in the United States is that Canada has a less extreme disparity of income distribution than has its neighbour. While south of the border, the bottom fifth of the population makes only 4.7 per cent of national income, in Canada the figure is 6.3 per cent. In the United States the top fifth of the population enjoys 42.7 per cent of national income, while in Canada it gets 38.9 per cent. As Richard Gwyn wrote in *The 49th Paradox*: "Canada is a middle-class nation, by no means as equalitarian as the Scandinavian ones, but far more so than the U.S."

If Canadian society places much higher value on the public funding of social programs, it accords military spending a much lower priority than does the United States. Among the seven major non-communist industrial countries, Canada spends the second lowest proportion, 2.2 per cent, of its gross national product (GNP) on defence, while the United States spends the highest proportion, 6.4 per cent.

If it is fair to conclude that Canadian society differs significantly from American society, is there any reason to believe that the Canadian way of life is threatened by a full free trade deal with the United States?

If the trade talks turned on the removal of tariff barriers to trade alone, there would be no such threat. However, the most significant aspect of the talks deal not with tariffs, but with the countless other ways that governments operate in society that can have an impact on exports and imports. It happens that the list of areas in which government has an impact is very long indeed.

As we have seen, U.S. negotiators have made it clear that what the Americans want in a trade deal is the achievement of what they call a "level playing field," that is, an economic environment in which the market is allowed to operate on its own. The problem is that the existence of Canada as a separate society in North America has always depended on large-scale government intervention in the economy. Without such intervention, we would not have built our railways, our telecommunications links, or the Trans-Canada Highway; we would not have established cultural institutions, such as the CBC and the National Film Board, to interpret our society to itself and the world.

If there is one thing that distinguishes the American way of life from all others, it is a singular belief in the ability of the market-place to set priorities for society. The United States has been the world's most perfect example of a society based on individualism. That has given the United States its great energy and its strong conviction that it has much to teach the rest of the world. All other developed western countries, including Canada, have believed in government intervention in the economy and the development of the welfare state to a much greater extent than has the United States. For Canada to go over to the concept of an economy with much more limited government intervention—in others words, "the level playing field"—is precisely to adopt that which is most central to the American way of life, and to give up that which has been central to our way of life.

Concretely, how could that affect us?

The many programs employed by government in Canada to bolster the economies of disadvantaged regions could be eliminated as a series of export-support measures. The payment of unemployment insurance to Canadian workers on a seasonal basis could be barred as an export-support measure.

In addition, the deal will mean that Canadian governments cannot use any direct means to Canadianize the ownership of industries or to attract or keep industry in this country as opposed to the United States. That would mean that our industries would operate in a completely American environment, in an economy fully integrated with that of the United States. And, in that context, the Canadian way of life has no chance. This country's more expensive social programs could wither, under the ceaseless pressure to keep our economy competitive with regions to the south where such programs are not in place.

Employers who do not want to contribute to such programs directly, or indirectly through taxation, could move their operations south to jurisdictions with less expensive programs. And our governments would have bargained away the right to stop them.

A way of life does not exist in a vacuum. It is the product both of the ideas and traditions of people and the institutional arrangements they make for themselves in their society. If we decide to adopt American institutional arrangements, let us not imagine that this will not affect our way of life.

We are already familiar with the American insistence that in trade talks between Canada and the United States "everything must be on the table." Clayton Yeutter, the U.S. Trade Representative, insists that "everything" includes cultural industries.

The American insistence on including cultural issues makes it clear that in the upcoming trade negotiations public policies to support Canadian culture could be attacked as barriers against the free importation of American culture—or, to use the jargon, as non-tariff barriers. Once on the table, such cultural supports could be eliminated or used as bargaining counters to help make a deal possible. In the fall of 1985, a secret memorandum, prepared by the External Affairs Department at the senior-deputy-minister level, proposed the possible use of Canadian cultural programs as "trade-offs" in the negotiations.

The seriousness of the cultural side of the talks became evident with the revelation in a leaked document authored by Allan Gotlieb, Canada's ambassador to Washington, that the giant U.S. firm Gulf + Western threatened a "scorched earth" policy if its takeover of the publishing company, Prentice-Hall in Canada, was blocked. Gotlieb advised his government to take the side of Gulf + Western or face serious rancour south of the border. In the days after the Gulf + Western affair, a large number of American congresspersons indicated they were prepared to go to bat to clear away Canadian restrictions on imported American culture. Eventually, as we have seen, the Gulf + Western takeover went ahead.

The Prentice-Hall issue was, of course, only the tip of the iceberg. The basic American concern had to do with the policy of the Canadian government, enunciated by Communications Minister Marcel Masse, that when foreign-based publishers decided to sell their Canadian subsidiaries, they should be required to sell them to Canadians. The purpose of the policy was to expand the 20 per cent share of the publishing market in Canada now held by Canadian-owned companies. It was also to expand the opportunities for Canadian authors, over 75 per cent of whose works are published by Canadian companies, despite their small share of the national market.

Moreover, beyond book publishing, there is the issue of film distribution in Canada, which is overwhelmingly controlled south of the border. For years it has been evident that Canadian film-making is seriously limited by the absence of major domestically owned film-distribution companies. Far more important to Gulf + Western than Prentice-Hall is its ownership of Famous Players in Canada.

Determined to scotch any renewed drive toward Canadianization of cultural industries, the United States deployed Secretary of State George Shultz, who lobbied External Affairs Minister Joe Clark on behalf of Gulf + Western when the two men met in Calgary in the fall of 1985.

Embarrassed by the leaked documents and by continuing American insensitivity on the issue, Canadian cabinet ministers, including the Prime Minister, have tried to make the cultural issue go away by proclaiming that Canadian cultural sovereignty will not be undermined in the talks. Such reassurances, however, have repeatedly been followed by U.S. statements that the cultural industries must be on the table.

Aside from the book publishing controversy, other cultural issues that could be at stake in the trade talks are:

- The controversial practice of inserting Canadian advertising into the cable signal from border U.S. television stations, protecting the territorial copyright the Canadian broadcaster has bought.
- The advertising tax write-off provision which promotes Canadian ownership of periodicals and which drove Time

Canada out of business and allowed *Maclean's* to operate as a weekly newsmagazine.

- Postal rate advantages for Canadian magazines.
- Tax support for films made in Canada.

The large-scale operation of the public sector in the cultural field in Canada, and restrictions on the operations of foreign-owned companies in the cultural field are viewed by Americans as limitations on the free operations of the market system in Canada. It is that issue — "the freedom of the marketplace" — that is the real bottom line in Canadian-American trade negotiations. The U.S. insistence on the removal of any interference with the market is for Americans not only an economic issue, but a matter of culture and ideology as well.

When Allan Gotlieb warned his government about the Gulf + Western issue, it was clear that much more was at stake than simply the fate of one book publishing company. The real issue was the way the U.S. administration and Congress would see Canada and Canadians. Gotlieb warned Ottawa in his confidential memo that if it pushed its publishing policy, the U.S. media could "infect the general perception of Canada as a destination for the U.S. investment dollar."

Since coming to office, the Mulroney government has gone to great lengths to make American law-makers see Canada as a country that respects the American way of doing things. The elimination of the National Energy Program, and particularly the replacement of the Foreign Investment Review Agency (FIRA) with Investment Canada have been aimed at changing the way Americans view Canada. Although during its years of operation FIRA blocked few foreign takeover bids, its very existence was seen as an offence to Americans. It was removed for symbolic reasons, for cultural reasons.

But in dealing with Americans, symbolism is of great importance. That is because of the special character of the United States as a country that takes ideology very seriously. For Canadians who have spent a great deal of time considering their own national identity, it is useful to consider how the American identity matters when it comes to negotiating a trading relationship.

The United States has a special history which separates it from the rest of the industrialized world, including Canada. American identity is rooted in the great revolutionary tradition of the eighteenth century, and the unparalleled American faith in individual freedom and the market-place.

At the core of the American reality is the fact that the United States is the product of the first modern revolution — a revolution, which like its Soviet counterpart, produced a messianic society, convinced that its ideas and institutions were founded on universal values that could liberate all mankind.

To a very considerable extent, the United States is a country with a "one myth" culture. The "one myth" that is central to everything in American life is the idea of individual freedom. American law is founded on the freedom of the individual, as is the American economic system. To Americans, the truths that are enshrined in their Constitution and Declaration of Independence are the central tenets in a national religion. To feel differently about such matters is to be un-American. Moreover, as the American sociologist Louis Hartz concluded, U.S. society has a paradoxical nature — it is the most liberal of societies, and yet it has a compulsive intolerance of ideological differences. While the British, the French, the Swedes, and the Canadians can have legitimate differences of opinion about the proper balance between the individual and society, between the market-place and government, for Americans these questions have a quasi-religious character that is born of revolution.

That the revolutionary tradition is very much alive today is seen clearly, and ironically, in the ideas of today's American neo-conservatives.

Irving Kristol, the godfather of American neo-conservatism, recently wrote in a new journal, *The National Interest*, about the conflict between American and Soviet messianism:

> In our own era, the distinction between religious ideas and political ideas is blurred.... We live in an era of 'ideologies' — of political ideas that breathe quasi-religious aspirations and involve quasi-religious commitments....

The basic conflict of our times—that between the USSR and the United States—is ideological.[56]

Kristol here is speaking approvingly, urging his fellow Americans to join the religious war against the Soviet Union—on behalf of American messianism. Messianism, of course, does not operate only against foes. It directs its compulsive message, on behalf of a way of life, especially effectively toward the citizens of friendly and smaller countries.

And so it is in the attitude of the U.S. government to trade negotiations with Canada. To Americans it is natural to demand that everything be put on the table in trade talks. After all, how else can one achieve the desired end—the dismantling of government intervention in the economy and society—so that free enterprise (the American way) can have unimpeded sway.

The Americans insist on discussing culture when they discuss trade, because for them there is a natural ideological dimension to the talks. The idea that a smaller country needs special measures to protect its identity does not resonate south of the border. Such an idea smacks of state intervention. It is an affront to the free working of the market system, and therefore to the American way of life.

It will be difficult for the Mulroney government, in the trade talks, to meet the clear Canadian desire for cultural sovereignty, if it wants to convince the Americans that we are prepared to do things their way.

Chapter Nine

The Death of Canadian
Conservatism

During the past decade, conservatism has been enjoying enormous intellectual and political momentum throughout the English-speaking world. Bored by the tired promises of the welfare state promoted by liberals and social democrats and feeling threatened by the competitiveness of East Asian economies, many people in the United States, Britain, and Canada have sought answers from a vigorous new conservatism.

One exponent of conservatism who has been receiving a good deal of attention in the United States and abroad, as we have seen, is Charles Murray, who believes that the welfare state has done enormous damage to society. I visited Charles Murray at his home in Washington, D.C., a two-storey dwelling, not far from the downtown area, protected by an iron security gate of the kind you expect on a jewellery store, not on a private residence.

Murray's theory is that the provision of welfare payments feeds the growth of a culture of dependency—spawning a prodigious increase in illegitimate births—creating a large segment of the population that cannot be integrated into the work ethic.

The solution to the problem for Murray is a simple one—let the market system do its job. Most of those who are able-bodied will find work if they have no choice, although a few may suffer.

What is important about Murray is not his precise formula for dealing with the poor, but the way he exemplifies the values of current American conservatism. For Americans, the rich texture of British-style conservatism, with its emphasis on tradition and the transmission of values from one generation to another, is almost entirely absent. Instead, American conservatism has been obsessed with the defence of the market system and free enterprise.

British conservatives, before the advent of Margaret Thatcher, always understood that their goal was to preserve a social system, not just to promote the free working of the market-place. They knew that, at times, the market system and free enterprise could create enormous dislocations, which ought to be offset by government. For them, there was not the automatic anti-government bias that has been so strongly associated with American conservatism.

Economists have never had much use for Canada. The reason is not hard to find. Canada has always been a barrier in the path of the full and unfettered operation of the free-enterprise, market system in North America. While Americans have been content to develop their economy largely through the private sector, Canadians have evolved a quite different relationship between the public and private sector.

It must be emphasized that the Canadian model of economic development has differed from that of the United States precisely because of the role the state played here as compared to the role played south of the border. For both practical and philosophical reasons, Canada never had the textbook market economy that most economists idealize. It must be emphasized at the outset that the role the state occupied in Canada was not an experiment in radicalism. In fact, it was an exercise in conservatism and pragmatism.

A country larger than the United States in area, with one tenth its population, needed an enormous concentrated effort to develop the infrastructure to link the country's regions into an effective whole. Without public money and the full backing of the federal government, the Canadian Pacific Railway would never have been completed in the 1880s. The Conservative government of John A. Macdonald had no qualms about using public money to finance the privately owned railway. Later, during World War I, a successor Conservative government took over two bankrupt railways and amalgamated them, creating the publicly owned Canadian National Railway.

Not only did Conservative governments find it philosophically acceptable to involve themselves in railways through public-private ventures, and through public ownership, it was a Conservative government that created the CBC, the Bank of Canada, and Trans-Canada Airlines in the 1930s.

This public-sector involvement on the part of Conservative governments took place at the provincial as well as the federal level. In Ontario, in the first decade of this century, the most remarkable public movement in support of public-sector involvement in the economy gathered strength under the broad auspices of the provincial Conservative party. The movement under the leadership of Adam Beck of London, Ontario, built support for public ownership of electric power utilities, leading to the establishment of the provincially and municipally owned Ontario Hydro system.

Conservative governments were prepared to use the powers of the state on behalf of economic development, both because it made good practical sense to them, but also because their brand of conservatism did not find it objectionable to do so.

Canadian conservatism cannot be described as having been highly articulate or systematic in its values. But what is crucial is that it did have a perception of the good that existed apart from the market-place. Canadian conservatism was imbued with the notion of nation-building, with the preservation of the best traditions of the past. It involved a clear sense of a Canada that was distinct and separate from the United States, a Canada that was to be a more ordered, stable society in which British ties were important. Canadian conservatism was born in reaction to the American revolution, against which it defined itself. In its great nineteenth-century manifestation it could never be reduced to being a simple defence of free enterprise.

The British historian A. J. P. Taylor describes the toryism

which was so important to Canada in the following way: "In essence, toryism rests on doubt in human nature; it distrusts improvement, clings to traditional institutions, prefers the past to the future."[57]

Nothing is more ironic than the ultimate redefinition of Canadian conservatism along the lines of American free enterprise republicanism, the force against which Canadian conservatives first defined themselves. American conservatism has never had the richer fabric of British and Canadian conservatism. The American revolution perfected the United States as the pure liberal, capitalist society—a society in which the market-place is the guarantor of freedom, and freedom is the only good. In a society such as this, order, stability, and community are sacrificed to the market. And since the market is ever-changing and volatile, it cannot serve as the guarantor of tradition or enduring human values. Only the preservation of the market itself can be seen as a conservative impulse—and this impulse alone is the only genuinely conservative feature in American conservatism. Moreover, to call the preservation of the whirlwind of the untrammelled market system conservative is to confuse uncontrolled change with order.[58]

Today's American conservatism, of course, does not exist in a vacuum. As a set of ideas, it is dedicated to the interests of American multinational enterprise and the strength of the U.S. state in a world in which American power is receding. American conservatives are forced to interpret a difficult world so as to justify the preservation of the American social and economic experiment as the most advanced in the world.

Canadian conservatives have adopted the American version of conservatism as their own at this problematic moment in U.S. history. For Canadian conservatives, there is a final irony. If conservatism has had an undeniable virtue in the past two centuries, it has been its insistence on the value of a sense of proportion in the face of demands for wholesale change. To a considerable extent this dimension of conservatism has taken the form of a cast of mind, a sensibility. Conservatives have characteristically resisted the logical on behalf of the sensible. What this means is that Canadian conservatism has played a valuable role in defending the existing community against proposals for social experiments.

Let us consider the proposition of wholesale free trade against this measure. According to neo-classical economists, free trade between Canada and the United States is the ultimate "logic" of the market system in Canada. Therefore, for theoretical reasons, to make the country conform to an ideal, the radical change must be made.

But is it sensible? Is it sensible to subject an entire social order to the prospect of serious wrenching and reordering in the name of a trade deal? Is it sensible to open trade negotiations with a superpower when your country already enjoys a huge trade surplus with that country? Is it sensible to choose the bilateral trade route over the traditional multilateral route, even though the multilateral route has long held the promise of helping balance Canadian trade away from overdependence on a single country?

The strange philosophical ground the government now occupies can be seen from the strident statements of the Prime Minister on the subject of free trade. Speaking in British Columbia in March 1986, Brian Mulroney launched a tirade against the opponents of free trade, describing them as "neo-reactionaries," "prophets of protectionism," and "apostles of the status quo." He pronounced that such people are "timorous, insecure and fretful" and that Canada can "trade its way to prosperity."[59] Here the Prime Minister is dressing himself in the garb of the daring man of change and painting his opponents as those who want to hang onto the Canadian past. There is much irony in this. In earlier days, Canadian conservatives would have understood how important it is to preserve the best of the past. Brian Mulroney does not understand this and does not know how to position himself creatively for the tough choices that must be made concerning the preservation of traditions and adaptations to a changing world. Instead he tries to will the problem away in blustering pronouncements that reveal that he is unsure of the ground he stands on.

What the government is doing is putting our nationhood, our sovereignty, on the bargaining table—and then deciding, in consultation with the Americans, which parts of it to keep. That is no way to run a country. As a strategy, it puts the maximum strain on Canadian society, forcing citizens to define what is most essential to them about their nationhood. And it does this in a process of mediation with a foreign government. Only an excess of fervent ideology could have driven the Mulroney government to such an extreme.

If we analyze the historic evolution of Canadian conservatism, we see that what is crucial is how the adoption of the notions of American neo-conservatism has altered the attitude of Canadian conservatives to the concept of nationhood. Traditionally, Canadian conservatives have placed a high value on nationhood, and have regarded the nation as more than the sum of its parts, as more than simply the aggregation of the individual interests of the Canadian population in the here and now. At its most impressive, Canadian conservatism exhibited a historical commitment to Canada, seeking to preserve the best of its past and to assure the country a future that grew out of that past.

Canadian conservatives like John A. Macdonald, although they were accused of colonial-mindedness, believed in the British connection as a counterweight to the power of the United States. Such conservatives were not opposed to Canada having a vigorous economic relationship with the United States, but they had a sense about where to draw the line in that relationship. They knew that if Canada drew too close to the United States, its national existence would be threatened. That fact has always been a given in Canadian life, a given which conservatives once understood better than anyone else.

Developing a small nation beside a superpower is never easy. Seeking balanced foreign relationships for such a country is always essential. Britain once served to provide such balance for Canadians. Now balance needs to be found in more far-flung relationships with Western Europe, with East Asia, and with the Third World. For earlier generations of conservatives, this kind of thinking would have been almost instinctive.

However, today's Canadian conservatives have lost their compass. By adopting American conservatism as their own ethic, they have allowed their fervent new commitment to the market system to obliterate their belief in anything else. As we have already seen, true believers in the market system have never had much use for Canada. How odd it is that today's Canadian conservatives have allowed themselves to be tempted by the 8 per cent solution—the willingness to trade sovereignty for the hope of a jump in our gross national product.

Chapter Ten

The Salesman

Simon Reisman, Canada's chief trade negotiator, has had a great deal of experience in the international economic arena. Born in Montreal in 1919, Reisman attended McGill University and later the London School of Economics. He entered the Canadian public service in 1946, when he went to work for the federal Department of Labour. That same year, Reisman switched to the Finance Department in Ottawa. During his long career in the federal service, Reisman specialized heavily in Canada's economic relations with other countries. He participated in the Canadian delegation to all sessions of the General Agreement on Tariffs and Trade and sat on the Royal Commission on Canada's Economic Prospects between 1955 and 1957, authoring the Commission's volume on Canadian-American relations. He served as the head of Canada's team for the negotiation of the Canada-U.S. Auto Pact in the mid-1960s. He reached the zenith of his career in the public service at the end of the 1960s when he became Secretary of the Treasury Board and later deputy minister of Finance, a position which he held until 1974.

During his years as the top civil-service adviser on the economy, he developed a reputation as a tough-minded fiscal conservative, who fought to hold the line on public spending in the eight federal budgets whose preparation he oversaw. When Reisman left the public service with a great deal of fanfare in 1975, he set himself up as an economic consultant, already regarded as a strong defender of the private sector.

Simon Reisman has always been a man for whom no project is too big, no task too daunting. He speaks his mind frankly, does not suffer fools gladly, and can always be expected to make the strongest possible case for his position on any issue.

In recent years, he has become seized of his most grandiose vision yet, the idea of selling gigantic quantities of Canadian water to the United States in what would be the biggest megaproject in the history of North America. For years the United States has been growing ever more thirsty for vast new infusions of fresh water. Water is needed to flush out the pollution-laden Mississippi system, now overburdened with the detritus of the industrial Midwest and to meet the demands of a growing population in the dry American Southwest.

Before being appointed as Canada's chief trade negotiator, Simon Reisman was personally associated with the Grand Canal Company as an economic adviser. The Grand Canal Company, as its name suggests, has been exploring the feasibility of feeding the fresh water from twenty rivers that empty into James Bay south into Lake Huron. From Lake Huron, the water would go through a continental grid system to feed the American Midwest and other parts of the United States with some of the flow going to western Canada.

This massive engineering scheme would work as follows: James Bay would be converted from a salt-water body to a fresh-water lake through the use of a sea-level dyke across the mouth of the bay. From James Bay, the fresh water would be pumped south through a system of canals, dams, and underground water tunnels. Existing rivers, the Ottawa and the French, would be engorged with huge additional quantities of water. Through Lake Huron would be pumped a volume of additional water equal to twice the flow of the Great Lakes system. Once in Lake Huron, the water would be available to quench the thirst of American industry.

When discussing the scale of the venture at a public meeting in the spring of 1985, Simon Reisman said:

The magnitude of the Grand Canal Project is some five times the size of the Apollo Moon Project, roughly 100 billion current dollars. It would take ten years to construct and put into operation... the construction of the project itself would produce for Canada about 150,000 direct jobs and at least as many again indirect jobs all over the country to supply the goods and services at all levels of sophistication to support this mammoth undertaking. It does not take too much imagination to visualize the array of machinery, equipment, vehicles, steel, cement, lumber, pumps, turbines, energy and the whole range of engineering, financial and other services that would be required for this project.[60]

According to Reisman's blueprint, virtually all of the capital for the project would come from the United States. Finally, for him the most important aspect of the project would be the "bargaining leverage" it would give Canada. Reisman stated:

I believe that this project could provide the key to a free trade agreement....

Do we have the courage and the imagination—yes, the audacity—to take on these two big projects, free trade and fresh water-sharing, at the same time?[61]

Simon Reisman is the latest in a long line of people who have been appalled at what they see as the utter waste involved in northern-flowing rivers that empty their fresh water into the sea. For them, northern Canada is a gigantic reservoir that can be tapped to serve the needs of American industry. In fact, in the opinion of many responsible geographers and environmentalists, the idea that northern-flowing water is "wasted" is a highly dangerous myth. They argue that northern Canada, while it holds huge reservoirs of water, also receives relatively low levels of rainfall. They warn that massive water-diversion schemes run the risk of significantly altering the climate in the north, not to mention reducing some areas of the country to virtual deserts.

The risk does not affect the north alone. The areas through which the water would be pumped include cities, towns, railways, highways, resort properties, and farms, all of which could be affected by the scheme.

From an environmental standpoint, the idea is chilling. From an economic standpoint, it reveals precisely the type of mentality which has underlain Canada's over-dependence on resource exports throughout its history. Simon Reisman's scheme brings new meaning to the old cliché about Canada as a "hewer of wood and drawer of water."

Just what would be the economic implications of this massive water export plan? As Reisman tells us, he envisions virtually all of the capital for the Grand Canal coming from the United States. The implications of a $100 billion inflow of American capital into Canada over a ten-year period are as gargantuan as are the implications of the southward-flowing torrent of water that is sought. The inflow would double U.S. investment in Canada.

It would have a further effect. When American capital flows into Canada, U.S. dollars are exchanged for Canadian dollars. What we are talking about is the most massive purchase of Canadian dollars in history, a purchase that would send the exchange value of the Canadian dollar soaring upwards, perhaps to a value higher than that of the American dollar. Considering that Reisman wants the water sale as a bargaining lever for free trade, the project would have an ironic result. With a much higher exchange value for the Canadian dollar, this country's exports would be priced out of world markets, in particular, the American market. Instead of opening the door for Canadian exports, "fresh water-sharing," as Reisman calls it, would slam the door shut for our export industries. It would make Canada much more dependent than it now is on the sale of resources, while making our manufacturing and service-sector exports much harder to sustain.

Simon Reisman's water scheme is, in all likelihood, a fantasy—a nightmare that will never come to pass. But his rapturous endorsement of the idea says something about his judgement. And what it says can be further seen by examining his broader ideas about the economy.

As far as Simon Reisman is concerned, a standard neoclassical view of the economy is all that is needed to understand how the world functions. The free market system is the best there is, and governments should stand aside to let it do its work.

In October 1976, Reisman outlined his theoretical ideas about the economy when he took on John Kenneth Galbraith in a debate sponsored by the *Financial Post*.[62] In his paper, Reisman rejected Galbraith's ideas, in particular, his view that capitalism has changed in recent decades due to the growth in power of giant corporations. Here Reisman was rejecting the insights in Galbraith's ground-breaking book, *The New Industrial State*.[63]

In that book, Galbraith argued that the economic system had evolved from an era in which competition prevailed to one in which the economy was divided into two parts: "the market system," in which small companies continued to be governed by the laws of competition; and the "planning system," in which a small number of corporations (no more than two thousand) had become enormously powerful in the key industrial sectors. According to Galbraith, corporations in the "planning system" had such power over costs, labour, and materials that they were able to substantially reduce risks and to free themselves from the full constraints of the market.

Naturally, if one accepts Galbraith's views about the growing concentration of power in the economy, the conclusion is clear that a relatively small number of powerful actors have the capacity to make decisions that will vitally affect such matters as where industries will locate, and the division of labour between people in different countries and regions. In such a world, the capacity of the state to counteract the power of giant corporations is the only means available to ordinary citizens to make sure that their basic needs are met.

Reisman rejects this Galbraithian cosmology. For him, the competitive model preferred by neo-classical economists explains reality better. In his debate with Galbraith, Reisman countered:

> I do not accept Galbraith's description of our economic system or his analysis of the way it functions.... All the available evidence indicates that the giant corporations—

however defined—which exercise a measure of market power occupy a considerably smaller area of the economy than Professor Galbraith suggests, no more than one-quarter at best.

Nor is there any evidence that the degree of corporate concentration—and hence of oligopolistic power—has increased significantly over the past decades in either the United States or Canada and thereby altered the basic structure of the economy.

Since Simon Reisman does not believe that giant corporations exercise great power in the economy, it follows that government power should be restrained. If government is not needed to offset the power of corporations, then the market system should simply be allowed to operate unimpeded. In this view of things, free trade makes perfect sense—it simply eliminates unnecessary barriers in the way of the market system. And since large multinationals do not have undue potential power, there is no need to worry about the decisions they will make in Canada once free trade is in place.

Following logically from this premise, Simon Reisman, in the speech he made linking water exports to free trade in the spring of 1985, called for the fullest possible free trade deal. He stated:

The agreement would provide for full national treatment of the goods, services and enterprises of the other—that is, identical treatment to that accorded to your own nationals. There would be virtually no exceptions, and the few that were agreed upon would disappear after a firm transitional period.

The implications of this view of free trade are very clear. Canadian governments would not be able to pursue "buy Canadian" programs to benefit domestic industry; programs undertaken to increase Canadian ownership of particular industries would be banned; and measures to protect Canadian cultural industries would be non-existent. In Simon Reisman's ideal world, the American "level playing field" is perfectly acceptable. For him, the American way of doing things is not a problem; it flows naturally from his own analysis of the world.

The only problem as far as Reisman is concerned is how to lure the United States into a free trade deal with Canada. And that brings us back to water exports. Reisman stated:

> A major difficulty, I fear, is that in economic terms the benefits from free trade are likely to be asymmetrical. U.S. industries already have their mass market, and the potential gains from new investment and improved productivity are certain to be less impressive. In the practical world in which we live Americans would, I suspect, have to see concrete benefits in other areas as well, if they are to accept the terms and conditions that Canadians would justifiably request in negotiations.[64]

The enticement for the Americans, as we have seen, would be massive Canadian water exports. The implications of Reisman's analysis is clear: without putting water exports on the table, the United States would be unlikely to be willing to make a deal favourable to Canada.

Simon Reisman's highly public stance, linking water exports and free trade only months before taking on the job of heading Canada's trade negotiating team, creates grave problems for the Mulroney government. And those problems are only enhanced by the fact that in 1983, while he was running for the leadership of the Progressive Conservative Party, Brian Mulroney expressed support for the Grand Canal scheme.

Chapter Eleven

The Alternative to Free Trade

At 2.00 p.m. on weekdays, except on Friday when it occurs at 11.00 a.m., parliamentarians gather in the House of Commons for Ottawa's version of blood sport—question period. The daily ritual keeps alive the perennial election campaign that never ceases in the nation's capital. The object of the opposition is to ask questions that inflict maximum damage on the government, and that win for party leaders that invaluable ten-second clip on the suppertime TV news that is the goal of so much political labour.

When political strategists in Ottawa are not planning for the daily skirmishes in question period, they are busy reading polls that tell them how their leaders are doing. All parties now pay a great deal of attention to polls and are guided by them in the language and substance of their day-to-day performance, although naturally the polls tell them not to acknowledge this too often.

What question period and the obsession with polls mean is that Ottawa politicians are a good deal more accessible to public opinion than citizens often believe. Whether or not it is a good thing to have a political system with so little concern for matters of strategic importance as opposed to tactics is a good question. One thing is clear, however; influencing the tone of the debate in Ottawa is not difficult. Citizens who care about the free trade issue need not despair. If they organize and make their views known and influence their fellow citizens, the politicians will listen and will alter their behaviour in response to pressure.

This is not to say that the Mulroney government has not committed itself very considerably on the free trade issue. As we have seen, in the fall of 1985, government officials confirmed the existence of a secret memorandum written in the Department of External Affairs at the senior-deputy-minister level on the domestic politics of Canada-U.S. trade talks.[65] The document outlined a strategy for keeping the debate on free trade low key, to avoid a backlash against it among Canadians. Government ministers were to stress how strongly existing programs protected Canadian sovereignty. For a government which regarded the communication of political matters as more important than the substance, the fact that a public relations strategy was in existence indicated just how far the Mulroney government was committed.

The Mulroney government can be moved from its present position, but only by clear evidence that a comprehensive trade deal with the United States is unpopular with Canadians. In addition, it must be evident that there is a viable alternative to free trade.

In asserting that a realistic alternative to free trade exists, it is unnecessary, in fact not desirable, to offer a blueprint for the Canadian economy. Instead, what is required is a statement of the principles on which an alternative economic strategy would be based. What follows is an attempt at such a statement.

First of all, Canadians need to learn from the key developments in the contemporary global economy as well as to learn from the best elements in their own past. The free trade choice would have Canada linked inexorably to the American economic model, a model which, as we have seen, is no longer on the cutting edge of economic advance. The alternative involves planning by business, labour, and government for the long range well-being of the country.

As we have seen, the most important development in the global economy over the past twenty years has been the evolution of a number of highly promising experiments in "national capitalism." While the countries carrying out these experiments differ widely in their cultural backgrounds and in their social policies, they all have combined both long-range strategic planning with competition. In the late twentieth century, with the long lead times needed for technological breakthroughs and new product development, this combination is particularly potent. It allows countries to seek out niches in the world economy where they can achieve excellence.

By rejecting free trade, Canadians would be keeping open the door for the pursuit of such a strategy. Ironically, this kind of strategy has many of the features, in principle, of the kind of mixed economy on which Canadian development was based historically. Having said this, however, we have no reason to be complacent in Canada. Making the Canadian economy competitive in international terms is an awesome task.

Canadians have a choice. They can be the victims of the international economic transformation that is underway. Or they can act between now and the end of this century to change their fate.

The nation's industries must be rebuilt to make them internationally competitive. Canada needs a technologically progressive industrial strategy. Rebuilding the country's key industries can only be undertaken if there is a transformation in the way Canadians think about themselves and their economy.

The attitudes that need altering are deeply ingrained. Canadians have never thought themselves capable of managing an independent economy. Three and a half centuries of making a living as a dependency of more powerful countries have left a deep mark. Canadians remain cautious, doubting their capacity to strike out on their own. In fact, throughout their history Canadians have never deliberately attempted to leave an economic empire. The people of New France only left the control of France as a result of the British conquest. The businessmen of the Province of Canada were thrown unceremoniously out of the old British mercantile empire in the 1840s when the mother country went over to free trade.

Today Canadians remain a dependency within the American economic system. And even though they have expressed a desire for more economic independence over the past fifteen years, it has not been a burning passion. Colonial-minded caution is still very strong in this country.

Changing the country's economic strategy, then, means unlearning a number of "truths" that have been taught us by traditional economists.

The first "truth" to be unlearned is that direct foreign investment creates jobs and leads to gains in productivity. The opposite is true. Foreign investment creates jobs abroad, leaving Canadians with fewer and lower-paying jobs. Foreign ownership is a major barrier to technological advance in this country.

The second "truth" we must unlearn is that there is necessarily an antagonism between government and the private sector in the running of the economy. The question must be asked directly: would Canadian business benefit from free trade with the United States or would it do better with an alternative economic strategy?

Many people have assumed that it is in the interest of Canadian business to favour free trade with the United States. In a narrow sense this assumption is often linked to the question of broader access to the American market for Canadian producers. However, as we have seen, there is already very wide access to the U.S. market for Canadian business. In practice, it is very difficult to find concrete examples of Canadian businesses that would expand their operations dramatically as a result of somewhat wider access to the U.S. market. In fact, of the many businesspeople I have spoken to in Canada over the past year, most say that they themselves would either be unaffected or negatively affected by free trade.

And yet, a very large number of Canadian businesspeople have supported free trade. Why? I have puzzled over this question for a long time, and have come to the conclusion that the reason has to do with the mind-set, the philosophy of Canadian business, rather than with any concrete sense of self-interest.

Spokespersons for Canadian business tend to make the automatic assumption that there is a natural antipathy between business and government. Free trade, then, is favoured by them as an extension of the free market system, as a way of further reducing the role of government in the economy. Such a sentiment, while quite natural in terms of the economic and political debates of recent years, ignores virtually the whole historical experience of business in relation to government in Canada.

Historically, Canadian business has depended very considerably on a partnership with government for its achievements. In fact, without such a partnership, the country would never have been opened up, the regions connected, and the infrastructure for resource extraction put into place. The business-government partnership created a national market that allowed both great firms and small ones to grow and flourish in Canada. Canada's actual economic history, as distinct from the fables of many of our economists, should set us straight. Creative economic development in Canada has always involved a blend of private and public-sector activity—sometimes through public-sector investment in privately owned operations, sometimes through the creation of crown corporations. Before the Tories in Canada became imitators of American Republicans, they created Ontario Hydro, the CNR, the Bank of Canada, and the CBC. Without such corporations and others, such as Petro-Canada, added since under Liberal governments, Canada would have fallen far behind in the establishment of an economic infrastructure capable of supporting an industrial economy. It is when we forget the experience of Canadians over the past century that we get into trouble.

Few serious analysts would challenge the contention that historically Canada's economy was built on the basis of a business-government partnership. And yet today, there is such an antipathy on the part of much of Canadian business to continuing to develop the tradition that made it strong. Nothing better illustrates the enormous impact of American ideas on Canada than this fact, that much of Canadian business is now willing to turn its back on its own experience in favour of the more "market-driven" approach of the United States.

The danger in this approach is that it will result in Canadian business being marginalized on the continent. Under free trade, some successful, lucrative businesses will be drawn into the centre of the U.S. market, much as Maritime banks were drawn into central Canada following Confederation. Such institutions will become more American than Canadian in their operations. Other Canadian companies will remain at home, specializing to penetrate selected target areas in the continental economy. Much of Canadian business will prove uncompetitive and will sell their operations to U.S. companies or will simply shut down. Once the link between business and active federal and provincial governments has been broken, the process by which new ventures receive the aid of the state will have been sharply curtailed. Canadian business will lose its autonomy, and its vigour, and will end up on the sidelines of the American economy.

What is needed instead is a new partnership between business and government in Canada, whose goal should be to make the country's economy internationally competitive in the late twentieth century—and this partnership needs to include labour. Only such a partnership would allow Canadians to engage in the critical combining of competitive market economics with long-term strategic planning that has proven so successful in East Asian and Western European economies.

Only in the English-speaking world is the notion of a partnership involving business, government, and labour a controversial idea. And, as we have seen, the English-speaking world has been far from setting the pace when it has come to advances in productivity over the past two decades. A new partnership can make Canadian business profitable and autonomous. However, such a partnership requires a basic change in the attitudes of Canadian entrepreneurs to other players in the economy.

Canada is too small and too far behind in the competitive battle of the late twentieth century to allow itself the luxury of ideological purity—either left-wing or right-wing.

This country must make use of all the available tools to transform the economy to serve the interests of Canadians.

Both the private sector and the public sector must be used to create productive jobs. Moreover, they must work together in combinations that are found advantageous.

Having now set out these general propositions, let us be more concrete, beginning with the manufacturing sector.

Canada's manufacturing sector needs to be rebuilt from the ground up. This task is the single most critical one in meeting the imperative of the technological transformation now underway. The effort needed must be national in scope, involving the federal and provincial governments, as well as the private sector.

To make this a national effort, Canadians in the Atlantic provinces and the West must be fully involved. The rebuilding of the manufacturing sector will require such a major effort that it cannot succeed if it is seen as a replay of the industrialization of the past—with manufacturing in central Canada feeding off the resources of the rest of the country.

Provincial governments in the West and the Atlantic provinces have always expressed a desire for the expansion of manufacturing in their regions. Decentralizing the location of manufacturing has now become a national necessity. Without it, the regions will be played off against each other and the multinationals will be the winners.

Canadianization is a key to rebuilding the manufacturing sector. Economic nationalism is an essential means to the end of establishing a technologically advanced and prosperous Canada.

Large pools of capital must be mobilized to create new Canadian enterprises and to retool existing ones.

To mobilize such capital, the federal government should undertake a new bond issue—call it a National Rebuilding Fund—to raise capital in the same way it now does with Canada Savings Bonds. The money for the fund would not be used for current government operations, including the retirement of the public debt. Instead it would be used to set up an investment pool of public money to create new corporations and to upgrade existing ones. Because of the historic, high rate of savings in Canada, billions of dollars could be mobilized in this way.

Canada's internal savings make it possible for the nation to pursue the vigorous rebuilding of the manufacturing sector. We have already examined the barriers that stand in the way

Savings in Canada

	Total Personal Income ($ bill.)	Personal Saving ($ bill.)	Saving % Personal Income	Undistrib. Profits ($ bill.)	Capital Allow. ($ bill.)	Gross Saving total ($ bill.)
1978	188.55	15.84	8.40	11.39	25.07	51.94
1979	210.73	18.05	8.57	18.05	27.95	64.36
1980	239.89	21.89	9.13	16.91	33.45	67.28
1981	287.48	32.12	11.17	11.29	40.56	84.49
1982	316.28	38.52	12.18	4.39	44.31	68.03

Compiled from Statistics Canada, *The Canada Year Book,* 1984.

of this kind of investment taking place. The problem is not lack of capital, as the accompanying table shows. In the late 1970s and early 1980s, as interest rates soared and as Canadians became fearful as a result of the economic climate, personal savings grew appreciably as a proportion of total personal income. In the mobilization of these savings, the government should turn away from policies of undirected fiscal stimulus in favour of investment in rebuilding the key goods-producing sectors of the economy.

A National Rebuilding Fund would not add to the nation's dead-weight debt. It would be the source of capital for productive and profitable investment. In the initial years, the carrying charges on the money would not be onerous. In later years, as the investments led to profits, the net result would be a surplus, not a deficit. Despite current new conservative rhetoric, public investment in productive activity is just as beneficial for the economy as private-sector investment.

Where would the money go? In sectoral terms, it would go into investment in those sectors of the economy where domestic and export markets have real potential. We should begin with sectors where Canada is now dangerously and unnecessarily dependent on imports.

The money would be invested in productive sectors of the economy. It would be invested in private companies, in joint ventures, and also in public-sector companies. Some examples of where it could be invested would be: in high technology manufacturing, to promote and underwrite Canadian efforts in microelectronics and in communications equipment; in the establishment of a world-scale mining-machinery complex in Northern Ontario; in the building of a steel-making and transportation equipment complex in the lower mainland of British Columbia; in the development of petrochemical, petroleum machinery, and agricultural equipment manufacturing in the Prairies; in the rebuilding of the aerospace industry in Quebec; and in the shipbuilding and fish-plant equipment industries in Atlantic Canada.

Just as there must be an expansion of public-sector enterprise in manufacturing, there must also be clear and workable incentives for Canadian-owned private-sector manufacturers. The Canadian private sector, like the American, has adopted a short-term, bottom-line approach to its operations. The result has been a poor record of innovation and, in recent years, very little improvement in productivity. Because the bulk of productive activity will remain in the private sector, it is critical to devise tools that ensure that capital investment there is sufficient and that it is geared to ends that serve the country.

Conservatives have an easy answer to this problem: let capital have complete freedom, in Canada and abroad, to be invested where the highest return can be made. If not enough capital is being invested, lower the tax rate on upper-income earners and on corporations. This will lead to the necessary investments being undertaken.

To a very considerable extent, this system is now in effect. It has not worked. Canadians have been prodigious savers. Somehow, though, their savings have not ended up as investments in the key areas needed to rebuild the manufacturing sector.

There is plenty of capital in Canada. It must be mobilized for socially useful purposes. In the private sector, capital can be streamed to where it will do the most good to reach the most enterprising entrepreneurs, who are key to new product development. Companies should be given corporate tax points off if they purchase Canadian machinery, carry out research and development, deploy new and more productive tech-

127

niques, train workers for skilled jobs, and encourage advancement for women.

Those who believe in an unfettered free market will strongly object to the notion of directing investment capital in this way. The fact is, however, that profits (the source of investments) are made through the work of society as a whole, not through the narrow efforts of the owners of capital. In a society as interconnected as ours, it makes perfect sense to insist that capital be invested to serve a useful purpose.

The rebuilding of Canadian manufacturing should be concentrated on a number of sectors: industries in which Canada has enjoyed success in the past and needs investment today to maintain that success (e.g., steel); industries where the country has huge and unnecessary trade deficits and where domestic production would be based on a large Canadian market now being serviced from abroad (e.g., machinery and auto parts); and industries that are bound to grow in the future as technological changes are introduced and where investments today can mean large markets in the future both at home and abroad (e.g., microelectronics and communications equipment).

In establishing a list of "winner" industries, there is the implication that there will be "losers." Politicians hate such lists because of their desire to be all things to all people. In general, however, Canadians are more realistic, understanding that in a world in flux some industries will flourish and some will decline. The truth about this must be faced and so too must the social necessity for protecting people from its impact.

Two kinds of positions on industrial and technological change are sterile: the one that decries the new techniques as destructive of human dignity and present employment patterns; and the futurist fantasy that sees machines as god-like saviours about to usher in an era of ease and plenty (or back to the Garden of Eden with a microcomputer). Changes are coming and cannot be stopped. Nations that debate this contention will not stop the new techniques. They will simply put themselves further down the list of industrialized nations in terms of the international division of labour. While obsolescent jobs can be

128

protected in the short run, the long-run consequence of this will be destructive of the living standard of the nation as a whole. Canada needs a general commitment to this proposition in a hurry. Only an agreement, involving both federal and provincial governments, labour, and business, can make this possible.

Given the splits in domestic business (between foreign- and domestically-owned components), effective leadership on the issue of technological change is unlikely to come from the business community as a whole. This is the case, despite frequent business rhetoric about the need to increase productivity. Given the nature of Canadian society, the log-jam on this issue has to be broken by the labour movement.

The labour movement ought to rethink its historical reliance on the adversarial system (bargaining with business, without sharing in industrial management.) Labour should insist on the need to rebuild the productive sectors of the Canadian economy. It should come out fully on the side of technological change and increased productivity. The deal it should extract from government and business for this should include: a commitment to the strengthening of social programs to allow workers to live decently during the transition; shorter hours with no loss in pay as productivity gains are made; programs for job retraining to prepare people to move from job to job and industry to industry, with society as a whole picking up the tab; and a rededication of the country to full employment, not as a rhetorical goal but as a real objective made possible by the rebuilding of the economy.

These are high objectives. Many would believe them unrealistic. The alternatives, however, are stark. Uncertainty about our industrial future will lead to the most sterile forms of job protectionism. The threat of the new conservatism will force people to dig in to protect themselves where they are now, whatever the consequences for the country as a whole. The alternatives lead to decline in international competitiveness and mean-spirited repression at home.

A new economic strategy involves not only the rebuilding of Canadian manufacturing but a new approach to the resource industries as well. The two sectors must be closely linked in the overall strategy.

One of the tragic consequences of the traditional pattern of Canadian economic development has been the creation of "one-industry towns," dependent on the extraction of one or a few resources. Such towns exist in every region of Canada. Their people were among the most desperate victims of the 1981-82 recession.

Sudbury, Ontario, is a good example of such a community. With a population of 100,000, Sudbury remains almost entirely dependent on the fate of world metal mineral markets, especially for nickel. During the decades when INCO dominated the world nickel market with the sale of Sudbury nickel (90 per cent of the non-Communist world's supply came from the Sudbury basin at the peak), no significant investment of the profits was made to diversify the economy of the region. The unavoidable happened. New sources of nickel were developed elsewhere. Armed with subsidies from their governments, foreign nickel producers cut into the world market share enjoyed by the Sudbury basin. Today, only half as many nickel-miners are working in the Sudbury mines as at the peak.

In typical Canadian fashion, Sudbury has been left to fend for itself. INCO, the great beneficiary of the community's labour, has been shifting its investments to new places and into new industrial fields as the Sudbury basin has gone downhill.

Although it is late for Canada to learn the lesson, it must be learned now. Federal and provincial governments must establish development funds from the sale of non-renewable resources. The funds must be reinvested in the communities as the ore is being depleted. Furthermore, in resource towns where the mineral is extracted overwhelmingly for export (such as Sudbury), the investment should not be made in the further processing or refining of the ore. This is dead-end investment, and it is highly capital-intensive. It creates few jobs and makes the community even more dependent on a single industry.

Diversification away from a single base must be the goal. Sudbury, for example, could become the location for the production of mining machinery, not only for domestic use but for export. Canada is the third largest mineral-producing nation in the world, and yet our deficit in trade in mining machinery approaches $1 billion annually. The market is here. It should be tapped to create jobs and to diversify the economic base of communities like Sudbury.

If the key to the resource-industry towns is diversification, we must also have an approach to the extraction and sale of the minerals themselves. Canadian minerals should be divided into two categories: those extracted largely for export and those for which there is a significant domestic market.

Strategies for minerals in the first category should be based on maximizing the rent on the sale of the resource abroad. If Canada's position in world production is strong, agreements should be sought with other producing nations to maintain high prices. Such an approach should be seen as short term to middle term. Instead of allowing most of the profits from the sale of the resource to go to private companies, governments should collect a very large share of the rents for reinvestment in the diversification of the economy in the resource-producing communities.

A different strategy is needed for minerals where there is a significant domestic market. Oil and natural gas are the most important resources in this category. Because petroleum remains (as it will for at least several decades) the key fuel that drives the Canadian economy, its availability is crucial to our future. A strategy is needed to allow Canadians to supply themselves with petroleum and to avoid, as much as possible, the sequences of boom and bust, shortage and glut that have characterized the petroleum industry.

Today we have a government that prefers a simple market-system solution to every problem. In the case of petroleum, such a strategy courts disaster in the long term. The reason for this is that a simple market system ignores the key realities that differentiate the petroleum industry from other industries.

According to the solution preferred by the Mulroney government, petroleum supply and pricing should be determined by the ebb and flow of the international petroleum market.

However, as everyone ought to know, there never has been a truly free international market with respect to petroleum. World petroleum has been dominated in recent decades by two forces, gigantic petroleum companies and the Organization of Petroleum Exporting Countries (OPEC). In the 1970s, as we saw in an earlier chapter, the oil companies and OPEC, in conjunction with the U.S. government, were chiefly responsible for the oil price revolution in 1973. In the period of rising world oil prices from 1973 to 1982, there was little relationship between the cost of producing petroleum and the wellhead price. The "world price," far from being determined by market forces, was determined by the ability of the OPEC cartel to restrict petroleum output through prorationing agreements among its members. OPEC simply produced far less oil than it could have, to keep the price high and rising.

In the early 1980s, however, OPEC was subjected to increasing strains. Oil markets failed to grow at previously predicted rates. The recession of 1981-82 resulted in a sharply depressed petroleum market. Moreover, non-OPEC producers, in particular the United Kingdom, Norway, and Mexico, were gaining an ever higher share of the world export market. OPEC countries had often cheated on each other in the past by producing more oil than they were allowed under the cartel's prorationing agreement. By the beginning of 1982, the cheating was getting out of hand. Too much oil was being produced to keep prices high. Nigeria (an OPEC member), Britain, and Norway took the lead in cutting prices.

Over the next several years, a weakened OPEC struggled to keep the cartel intact. By the winter of 1986, that effort failed and the price of oil began a free fall to $15 (U.S.) a barrel. Underlying the plunge in prices in 1986 was the complete failure of the cartel's prorationing. Under the circumstances, Saudi Arabia, the OPEC member with the greatest financial clout and production capacity, decided to teach other OPEC and non-OPEC exporters a lesson. Saudi Arabia turned up its production of oil to speed the fall in price.

The strategy of the oil-rich kingdom was simple: by flooding the world with cheap petroleum, Saudi Arabia was hoping to undercut countries with higher production costs, to cause projects for the development of high cost petroleum to be cancelled or delayed, and to regain a higher share of international petroleum markets. Once having driven the higher-cost producers out of the market, Saudi Arabia hoped it would be able to impose peace on the world's oil exporters in the form of a refashioned OPEC with an effective prorationing system. In other words, Saudi Arabia hoped to turn the mid-1980s glut into a shortage as soon as possible so that a new oil price revolution would be possible.

By the time the Saudi Arabian strategy was underway in the winter of 1986, the federal government had moved to deregulate the price of oil and natural gas and had replaced the Petroleum Incentive Program (PIP) grants to Canadian-owned oil companies (for exploration and development activities) with a tax-based incentive system. What this meant was sharply reduced cash flow for oil producers in Canada as the world price of oil dropped and, as a consequence, sharply reduced budgets for petroleum exploration and development.

Unfortunately, the short-sighted policy of deregulation is almost certainly consigning Canada to the dislocation of sharp energy price rises, and even potential energy shortages, in the 1990s, when the price of petroleum is expected to rise again. Canadians should have learned by now that the petroleum industry has given us repeated bouts of shortage and glut, boom and bust. This is evident in Alberta, which grew at a phenomenal rate between 1973 and 1982. Since 1982, however, the province has suffered serious economic dislocation, first as a result of the recession in 1982 which coincided with falling world oil prices and then, even more, from the drastic plunge in world petroleum prices in the winter of 1986.

The folly of boom and bust can be seen in the fact that Albertans today continue to suffer high unemployment, as they watch their property values fall and their businesses put at risk. An intelligent economic policy would cushion society against these extremes. Canada ought to impose a tax on cheap imported petroleum and ought to invest the money in the exploration and development of the petroleum reserves the country will require in the next decade. In addition, Canadian consumers should be asked to pay a few cents a litre more for gasoline now, to provide funds for grants to private-sector Canadian-owned petroleum companies and to Petro-Canada to give the industry the means to go ahead with expensive projects. Without such initiatives, Canadians will, in all likelihood, be subjected in the 1990s to the same wrenching debates they experienced in the 1970s, as producing and consuming provinces do battle in a period of renewed oil-price increases.

The overall objective of manufacturing and resource strategy should be to end Canada's undue dependence on the extraction of raw materials for exports. The notion of the new conservatives, that it is not so bad to be "hewers of wood and drawers of water," after all, should be firmly rejected.

Over a very long period, the proportion of Canada's gross national product accounted for by goods-producing industries has been declining. The decline parallels a similar decline in other industrialized countries. There is evidence that the shift from goods-producing to non-goods-producing industries has been a factor in declining productivity in Canada. One of the objectives of Canadian economic policy should be to maximize the potential for goods production in the Canadian economy, both by aiming to produce a higher proportion of the goods consumed in Canada and by increasing the country's goods-exporting capability.

Canada's economic strategy for the future must be human-centred, not raw-materials-centred as it has been in the past. The key resource for Canada's future must be its people, the development of the nation's human and creative potential. This perspective can link approaches to the goods-producing and non-goods-producing sectors.

Most Canadians, about 70 per cent of wage and salary-earners, work in the so-called service sector of the economy. They work for banks, insurance companies, merchandising operations, and in education, health care, and private and public administration. Many of them work for governments.

Such people often find it difficult to believe that the fate of their sector of the economy depends very much on the health of commodity production. But it is so. If they work in the merchandising of products, their relationship to the commodity-producing sectors is obvious. Even if they work for banks or insurance companies, the relationship is very direct. The financial institutions of Canada have always had their base in the nation's commodity production. For educators and health-care professionals, the relationship is less direct, but nonetheless very real. Without the surplus generated in goods production, the revenues to sustain the educational and health-care systems would not be there.

In a vibrant economy, there is a complex interaction between goods-producing and non-goods-producing sectors. Just as the surplus to sustain education and health care comes from goods production, without the provision of education and health care, the goods-producing industries would wither.

If Canada's goal is to train its people to realize their potential in the work force (and more broadly as human beings), a very high priority must be given to the non-goods-producing sectors. Allowing the training and education of Canadians to be eroded for short-run reasons of economy, as provincial governments are now doing, is penny-wise and pound-foolish.

Training people will not create jobs. But in the context of a strategy to rebuild the goods-producing industries, training becomes critical. In an era of high unemployment, Canada must train its own people to do skilled jobs, not simply import them as it has in the past. Today in the United States the training of young people, to make the American economy competitive, has become a very live political issue. It is a no less important issue for Canadians.

The training of Canadians to do skilled jobs raises the issue of decision-making in the economy. Political democracy in Canada has never been matched by economic democracy. This is true not only in relation to income distribution; it is true in respect to the system of production itself. The industrial system in this country has been authoritarian in structure. It has relied on the transmission of simple instructions down the chain of command to production workers. Workers on the production floor have been valued, not for their capacity to think

135

or to innovate, but for the ability to carry out instructions from on high.

Democratization of the workplace is now essential to the successful transformation of the productive sectors of the economy. If the goal of Canada's human resources policy should be to train the work-force for highly skilled tasks, then our industrial structure can no longer be allowed to remain authoritarian. A rigid, top-down system of command in industry will negate the contribution a skilled work-force can make to the way things are done.

Not only does the trade union movement need to be involved in "industrial strategy" at the macroeconomic level, it needs to be involved at the level of decision-making in the workplace.

In the period of rapid change through which we are now passing, Canadians have fundamental choices to make. The most basic choice of all concerns our view of human nature — of what motivates people and of what the purposes of social and economic organization should be.

Canadians can give in to the present climate of fear and choose the mystical option of the new conservatism, an option based on a debased conception of humanity, on the notion that the vast majority of people can only be motivated through fear.

There is another choice, however. It is the humanist choice. At bottom, it is based on a different conception of people, one that believes that creativity is linked to co-operation, not selfishness — that the human capacity for innovation is not limited to a few entrepreneurs but exists in the population at large.

In the final analysis, debates about economic strategy have always been debates about the kind of society we desire. In a conservative economic order, there is an ultimate distortion of means and ends. In it, the vast majority of people are a means to the end of economic progress — with only a few titans being fully human actors. In a humanist economic order, the economy is a means, and nothing more than that, for the realization of human goals. Only in this framework can values outside of economic productivity for its own sake have meaning. Today such values are of vital importance—the preservation of the environment and the pursuit of peace being the two most important examples.

Free trade with the United States, as we have seen, amounts to a Fortress North America strategy vis-à-vis the rest of the world. The alternative to free trade also involves a stance with respect to the rest of the globe, but it is one in which Canada deals with other nations as a viable, national economic entity. Canada has been a member of the General Agreement on Tariffs and Trade (GATT) from its founding in the late 1940s. Canada has a stake in continuing to expand the global trading system, as it should now be doing by adding its weight to the movement for a new round of GATT talks.

We have analyzed the weakness of the American economy and its increasing inability to deal with the challenge of national capitalist systems which combine individualism and competition with the capacity for long-range strategic planning. The American economy can only approximate this potent combination of qualities, so essential to success in the late twentieth century through the massive military sector of its economy. The military route is highly inefficient and indirect, leaving the United States unadaptive against its economic challengers, principally those in Asia.

It is clear, as we have seen, that entering a free trade arrangement with the United States means moving over to a more "market-driven economy." This means an economy in which strategic long-range planning is less, not more, possible. It means moving over to the American system at exactly the moment in history when that system is revealing its fundamental weakness. There could be no greater economic folly for Canada, no greater misreading of the history of our time.

Notes

The discussion on American border states in Chapter Two, and much of the material in Chapter Eight first appeared in a series of articles in the *Toronto Star* on January 25, 26, and 27, 1986. Grateful acknowledgement is made to the *Toronto Star* for their permission to use this material.

1. Lester Thurow, *Dangerous Currents: The State of Economics* (Vintage Books, 1984), p. xviii.
2. Economic Council of Canada, *Ninth Annual Review, The Years to 1980,* 1972, p. 36 and p. 68.
3. Statistics Canada, *The Canada Year Book,* 1985, p. 173.
4. Canada, Department of Energy, Mines and Resources, *An Energy Policy for Canada—Phase 1* (Ottawa, 1973), vol. 1, pp. 102, 103.
5. See the *Report of the Royal Commission on the Economic Union and Development Prospects for Canada* (Supply and Services Canada, 1985).
6. Ibid., vol. 1, p. 375.
7. *The Globe and Mail,* February 28, 1986.
8. *The Globe and Mail,* February 18, 1986.
9. I visited Frank Lumpkin in September 1985, while doing work for a National Film Board series on Canada and the world economy.
10. The figures that follow in this chapter on the border states were compiled from the *New York Times,* April 29, 1985, and *The U.S. Statistical Abstract* (Bureau of the Census, 1985).
11. The figures for Canada in this chapter were compiled from *The Canada Year Book* (Statistics Canada, 1985).
12. For a more detailed discussion of the oil-price revolution, see, James Laxer, *Oil and Gas* (Lorimer, 1983).
13. Robert H. Hayes and William J. Abernathy, "Managing Our Way to Economic Decline," *Survival Strategies for American Industry* (Harvard Business Review, 1983), pp. 15, 16.
14. Ibid., pp. 18, 19.
15. Ibid., pp. 18, 19.
16. Ibid., p. 29.
17. Robert H. Hayes and David A. Garvin, "Managing as if Tomorrow Mattered," Ibid., p. 39.
18. Hayes and Abernathy, Op. Cit., p. 28.

19. Robert B. Reich, *The Next American Frontier* (Times Books, 1983), pp. 64-66.
20. For a discussion of the potential of flexible systems production to challenge traditional industrialism, read Michael Piore and Charles Sabel, *The Second Industrial Divide* (Basic Books, 1984).
21. Robert Reich, Op. Cit., pp. 117-39.
22. Ibid., pp. 3-21.
23. Lester Thurow, "A Time to Dismantle the World Economy," *The Economist,* November 9, 1985.
24. *New York Times,* November 18, 1984.
25. Mike Davis, "Reaganomics' Magical Mystery Tour," *New Left Review*, Winter 1985.
26. Ibid.
27. International Monetary Fund, *World Economic Outlook,* April 1984, p. 8.
28. John Eatwell, *Whatever Happened to Britain,* BBC, 1983, see discussion in Chapter 5.
29. *New York Times,* November 18, 1984.
30. Ajit Singh, "The Long-Term Structural Disequilibrium of the U.K. Economy: Employment, Trade and Import Controls," a paper presented at the University of Modena, November 1982.
31. *Toronto Star,* March 9, 1986.
32. *The Globe and Mail,* April 1, 1986.
33. B. W. Wilkinson, "Some Comments on Canada-U.S. Free Trade," *Canada-United States Free Trade* (University of Toronto Press, 1985), p. 95.
34. *The Globe and Mail,* February 28, 1986.
35. Ibid., February 16, 1986.
36. Ibid., February 15, 1986.
37. Ibid., April 24, 1986.
38. This "wish list" is compiled from statements by U.S. government officials, the writings of Canadian free traders on the terms Canada will be asked to consider, and the projections in federal and provincial government studies of what the U.S. government wants from Canada.
39. *The Globe and Mail,* February 19, 1986.
40. For a discussion of currency arrangements and international trade, read Jeffrey Garten, *Foreign Affairs,* Winter 1985.
41. *The Globe and Mail,* March 1, 1986.

42. For an excellent summary of the factors underlying the rise of East Asia see, Roy Hofheinz and Kent E. Calder, *The Eastasia Edge* (Basic Books, 1982).

43. Statistics Canada, *Economic Review,* April 1985.

44. Ibid.

45. Ibid.

46. *Toronto Star,* March 9, 1986.

47. Lester Thurow, "A time to dismantle the world economy," *The Economist,* November 9, 1985.

48. Gordon Laxer, unpublished paper on the West and free trade, 1985.

49. Ibid.

50. *The Globe and Mail,* February 19, 1986.

51. Simon Reisman, "Canadian Trade at a Crossroads," unpublished paper presented at a conference of the Ontario Economic Council, April 16-17, 1985.

52. Anthony Westell, "Economic Integration with the U.S.A.," *Perspectives,* Winter 1985.

53. *The Globe and Mail,* March 4, 1985.

54. Ibid., June 9, 1984.

55. The figures on violence in the United States and Canada are compiled from *The U.S. Statistical Abstract* (Bureau of the Census, 1985), and *The Canada Year Book* (Statistics Canada, 1985).

56. Irving Kristol, *The National Interest,* Fall 1985.

57. A. J. P. Taylor, *Essays in English History,* "Tory History," (Penguin, 1976), p. 18.

58. For a discussion of the differences between Canadian and American conservatism, read George Grant, *Lament for a Nation* (McClelland and Stewart, 1965).

59. *Toronto Star,* March 9, 1986.

60. Simon Reisman, "Canadian Trade at a Crossroads," unpublished paper presented at a conference of the Ontario Economic Council, April 16-17, 1985.

61. Ibid.

62. Simon Reisman, unpublished paper, presented to Financial Post conference, October 1976.

63. John Kenneth Galbraith, *The New Industrial State* (New American Library, 1967).

64. Simon Reisman, Op. Cit., paper presented to Ontario Economic Council.

65. *The Globe and Mail,* November 6, 1985.